WEST MIDLANDS ROCK

PRJ Harding climbing at Pontesford Rocks. Photo: A J Moulam

WEST MIDLANDS ROCK

by

D.Kerr

CICERONE PRESS

MILNTHORPE, CUMBRIA

Second Edition
© D.Kerr 1995
ISBN 1 85284 200 8
First Published 1988
ISBN 1 85284 018 8

ACKNOWLEDGEMENTS

I would like to extend my thanks to everyone who helped directly, or indirectly, with the first edition. It has proved very much easier to produce this edition as I have been able to concentrate on those areas which needed change or improvement in order to produce what I feel is a better and more accurate final product. This would not have been possible without all of this initial help.

A big thanks must go to Peter Stacy who, over the years, has given me tremendous support and encouragement. More recently, Peter has worked behind the scenes in liaison with the B.M.C, The National Trust, Shropshire County Council, The Hardwick Estate and numerous other interest groups to achieve suitable and practical access agreements for Ippikins Rock, Llanymynech Quarry, Grinshill and Nesscliffe. Thanks also for your company on some superb days on the crags, and for making me laugh when I shouldn't really have been taking things so seriously!

Steve Adderley has helped with the production of the manuscript; spending endless hours sitting at the keyboard when he certainly should have been doing something more constructive. Thanks for your time and your patience Steve. Gary Gibson has given constructive help and criticism; the contents of this guidebook have also expanded somewhat as a result of his labours!

Many others have helped in one way or another; Brian Phillips, Tony Moulam, Peter Moulam, Roger Lanchbury, Edwin Smith, Adam Brown, Ian Smith, Andy Popp, Nick Dixon, Nick Postlethwaite, John Codling, Stuart Bickel, Roger Smith, Paul Harrison, Walt Unsworth, Chris Gilbert, Roger Bennett, Bill Wright, Cath Pyke, Stan Wintrip and John Neil.

Finally, I should like to dedicate this guide to Karen, my fiancé who has shown me that there is rather more to life than simply climbing and perhaps I should now be thankful as I certainly won't be updating it again!

Front cover: Varsity Buttress, Pontesford Rocks
Climber: Doug Kerr Photo: Simon Grove/Kerr Collection

CONTENTS

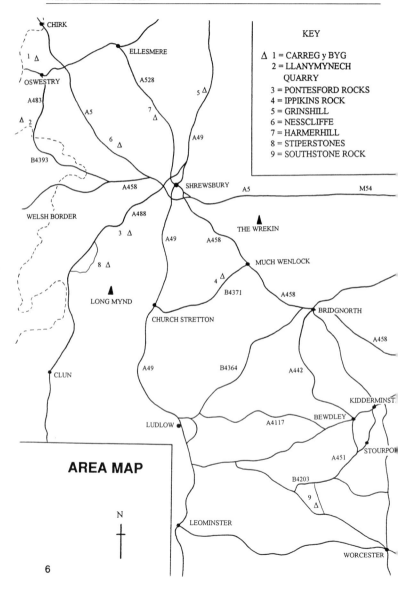

KEY

Δ 1 = CARREG y BYG
2 = LLANYMYNECH QUARRY
3 = PONTESFORD ROCKS
4 = IPPIKINS ROCK
5 = GRINSHILL
6 = NESSCLIFFE
7 = HARMERHILL
8 = STIPERSTONES
9 = SOUTHSTONE ROCK

AREA MAP

N

6

INTRODUCTION

Since the production of the first edition in 1988 there have been some interesting developments on the crags of the West Midlands. The guide certainly made a wide variety of climbers aware of the possibilities and it is pleasantly surprising to see several of the crags taking on a degree of local popularity; this is to be encouraged and will hopefully be consolidated with this second edition.

Several of the crags have seen plenty of new route activity. Llanymynech Quarry now has a wealth of new and mainly sports climbs to tempt climbers from much further afield. This quarry should become firmly established as a very worthwhile venue, which is especially recommended for the winter months; it is reasonably sheltered and takes very little seepage during periods of wet weather. To reflect the changing demands of climbers, the sports climbs at Llanymynech Quarry have been given a French grade alongside the standard 'E' grade and technical grade.

The sandstone crags have also seen plenty of activity. Further information has come to light for routes at Grinshill. Nesscliffe now has impressive new routes of a generally high order of difficulty. All of this information is now documented and will hopefully serve to entertain and inspire climbers over the next few years. There certainly remains plenty of scope for further development.

In an attempt to provide some historical interest and also to give credit to those who have contributed routes to this guide, I have compiled details of first ascents at most of the crags. Unfortunately, this has not been possible for all of the crags; it would be an extremely difficult task at Grinshill. Comments, alterations and corrections are to be welcomed in an attempt to bring these records up to date. I would be particularly interested to hear of further details concerning the early days at Pontesford

Rocks and Nesscliffe. So please write directly with any details to CICERONE PRESS, 2 POLICE SQUARE, MILNTHORPE, CUMBRIA. I have also compiled separate graded lists for most of the crags which are not intended to be taken too seriously!

Unfortunately, there have been some access difficulties. In hindsight this was rather predictable with the sudden arrival of quite large groups of climbers at relatively obscure venues. Please read the notes on access in the introduction to this guide as well as the relevant section for each crag. At all times please use your common sense; remember that poor or irresponsible behaviour will do little to further the interests of the climbing community.

For this edition it was decided not to include details of Castle Rock at Cleeve Hill as it does not really fall within the scope of the West Midlands. Instead, this edition concentrates on those crags within Shropshire and Worcestershire, with the bulk of the worthwhile climbing concentrated in Shropshire, or very close to it! Unfortunately, both the quality and quantity of available climbing in Worcestershire leaves a lot to be desired. The routes described at Southstone Rock and the Malverns, although worthwhile, are really only of interest to the local climber with some spare time on his hands.

With regard to the layout and format of the guide, the crags within each section have been described working from north to south. The format used by the Peak District guides has been used in the description of each crag to provide details of situation, access, character and approach. As many crags are likely to be relatively new to climbers, particular attention has been given to details of the situation and the approach and hopefully the guide contains enough useful information to enable the climber to reach the crags without reference to road maps. For those climbers seeking out some of the more esoteric minor crags, then Ordnance Survey maps may prove to be useful. The relevant sheets of 1:50,000 Landranger Series are;

Sheet 126	Shrewsbury
Sheet 127	Stafford and Telford

The future of this publication now seems to be assured as a result of recent developments, indeed, at a couple of the crags, the state of present development represents only 'the tip of the iceberg'. On the other hand, one of the personal attractions of the area has been the peace and solitude that some of the crags have been able to offer at times when the crags of the Peak District or North Wales have been filled to capacity.

TECHNICAL INFORMATION

GRADING SYSTEM

The standard adjectival grading system has been used up to and including Hard Very Severe. Beyond this the E grade has been used. Technical grades for pitches of 4A and above have been used in conjunction with this adjectival grade.

Please note that at Llanymynech Quarry, the new sports routes have also been given a French grade alongside the E grade and technical grade. It is assumed that this information will be self explanatory to those who are repeating these routes. This system certainly helps the climber to quickly identify those sports climbs which rely upon fixed protection.

If a pitch uses some aid, then the number of points required is indicated after the adjectival grade. If a pitch consists purely of aid climbing then the artificial grades of A1, A2 etc. have been used.

SANDSTONE GRADING

Grinshill and Hamerhill

In view of the unpredictable nature of the rock and in the absence of reliable natural protection, the routes are graded simply in terms of their technical difficulty, often with the indication of NL (Not Led). These routes are intended as top rope problems unless at a later date they are either led or soloed. Obviously the climber is free to decide whether to top rope, lead or solo. It is imagined however that this information will be only of minority interest as leading on sandstone can be a very serious affair. This grading system allows for flexibility as routes are included that would otherwise be omitted. It has been used effectively in other areas of the country and adequately reflects the problems of sandstone climbing.

Nesscliffe

At Nesscliffe the recent trend has been for lead ascents of the majority of the new routes, often after careful preparation. There has also been an increasing trend for lead ascents of established routes which have sufficient natural or fixed protection. To incorporate this information, the adjectival grade (ie; the E grade) for on-sight ascents of all routes which have been led, are now included after the technical grade. PLEASE NOTE, this system is not designed to encourage on-sight ascents at Nesscliffe as leading on sandstone remains a serious business and the climber is free to decide whether to lead, top-rope or solo.

Taking into account the grading system used for Grinshill and Hamerhill it is inevitable that such a 'dual standard' system will attract criticism and possibly even cause confusion to users of this guide. However, this approach does go some way towards reinforcing the character of the sandstone crags with Nesscliffe being a serious 'hard mans' crag and Grinshill a more friendly 'something for everyone' venue.

ROUTE QUALITY

A system of 'stars' is used to indicate the quality of the routes. On all the crags the standard 'three star' system has been used. This helps to indicate the quality of the routes as follows;

*	Good
**	Excellent
***	Superb

It is worth noting that there are a large number of routes, which although not awarded 'stars', provide worthwhile climbing.

The symbol '+' has been used to denote a route which has not been checked or where details or the grade have not been confirmed. Climbers are therefore required to use their own judgement when approaching such routes.

NEW ROUTES

Please forward details of any new routes to Cicerone Press, 2 Police Square, Milnthorpe, Cumbria. This is essential if records are to be kept up to date. Comments on existing routes or inaccuracies within the text are also welcomed.

ACCESS AND CONSERVATION
by Peter Stacey

The crags and outcrops within this guidebook cover some of the most beautiful and fragile areas in the West Midlands. Like many other parts of the countryside where climbers play, access and conservation increasingly come into the equation when deciding where to spend a day's climbing. Many hours have been spent in trying to resolve multiple difficulties and to ensure that the most satisfactory solution available to all parties concerned has been reached. This has not always been to the benefit of climbers and we have had only ourselves to blame on several occasions where restrictions have now been imposed. We all therefore bear a collective responsibility to ensure that we do nothing to jeopardise access agreements.

The access situation for crags in this guidebook have been checked as far as possible with the relevant landowners and authorities. THIS IN NO WAY IMPLIES ANY RIGHT OF ACCESS TO CLIMB AT ANY CRAG. Climbers should check that there have been no alteration to access agreements. Such alterations will be published in the climbing press, the B.M.C. access news sheets and in local outdoor shops. In particular, the agreements for Ippikins Rock, Grinshill and Llanymynech Quarry are of particular importance. These agreements are comprehensively covered in the relevant sections and need to be strictly adhered to.

There is a wealth of interesting flora and fauna in this area for everyone to enjoy in addition to the climbing. Shropshire is geologically diverse with various limestone, sandstone and volcanic rocks within its borders. This variety is reflected not only in different climbing styles, but also in a wide range of plants and wildlife, many of which are subject to protection under the 1981 Wildlife and Countryside Act. This protection can be, and often is, enforced by penalties arising from criminal prosecution. Climbers generally have a history of abiding by access agreements and behaving in a way which helps to protect the crag environment. However, the following general points should always be taken into consideration along with any points made specific for each crag.

1. Check for alterations to access agreements either in the climbing magazines, by contacting the B.M.C, or the Midlands Area Access Officer.

2. Take all litter home, including chalk wrappers, finger tape, broken laces etc. Please take home any litter you find and leave the crag cleaner than you found it.

3. Keep to the approach described, unless notified otherwise. Short-cuts over walls or fences will result in the loss of local goodwill. Be sensible when parking.

4. Respect the right of others to enjoy the countryside. Shouting, foul language or other anti-social behaviour are unacceptable.

5. The B.M.C. spends much time, effort and money in sorting out access problems. Many climbers take their freedom for granted and often without considering the hours that both local volunteers and national staff put in to maintain access or to resolve problems. Please support them. If you encounter an access problem contact either the Midlands Area Access Officer or the Access Liaison Officer at;

> The British Mountaineering Council,
> 177-179 Burton Road,
> West Didsbury,
> Manchester
> M20 2BB
> Telephone 0161 445 4747
> Fax: 0161 445 4500

ORGANISED GROUPS

Unfortunately, access agreements have been complicated by the use of several of the crags by organised groups. In particular, at Ippikins Rock the National Trust are very concerned at the damage that has occurred as a result. As part of the new access agreement the National Trust have therefore requested that organised groups DO NOT USE the crag. Similarly, the Hardwicke Estate have requested that Grinshill is not used by organised groups. At other crags, Carreg y Byg for example, current access arrangements could be jeopardised with persistent use by organised groups. Several crags have a history of group use and are therefore more suitable sites; **High Rock** at Bridgnorth, **Cul-de-Sac Quarry** at Llanymynech, **Pontesford Rocks** and **Fairy Glen Quarry**.

FIRST AID

In case of accident;

1) SUMMON HELP/EMERGENCY SERVICES. Dial 999 in the first instance.

2) IF SPINAL INJURIES or HEAD INJURIES are suspected DO NOT MOVE THE PATIENT without skilled help, except to maintain breathing.

3) IF BREATHING HAS STOPPED, clear airways and commence artificial respiration. Do not stop until expert opinion diagnoses death.

4) STOP BLEEDING BY APPLYING DIRECT PRESSURE.

5) KEEP THE PATIENT WARM.

Shropshire

CARREG Y BYG

OS Ref: 248324 Sheet 126 (1:50,000 Landranger Series)
With assistance from Bryan Phillips

CHARACTER

Carreg y Byg is a small and sheltered limestone quarry lying four miles to the north-west of Oswestry. The quarry is surrounded by a canopy of trees and is therefore rather slow to dry after rainfall, though most of the quarry walls benefit from any afternoon sun during the summer. During periods of dry weather, the quarry is a useful and increasingly popular venue for local climbers. Visitors from further afield will be pleasantly suprised; the quality of the rock on the popular routes is very good as regular traffic has helped to keep the climbs free from loose material and vegetation. However, the climber will be required to exercise some caution when approaching the more obscure routes and some care should be taken on the finishes of most of the routes.

Numerous trees and fence posts offer reliable and often very convenient belays at the top of the climbs and are also useful for top-roping purposes. The quarry contains a number of worthwhile routes but it would certainly benefit from increased traffic or the further careful attention of local enthusiasts. There is still potential for further new routes of all grades.

ACCESS

Please remember that the quarry lies on private land. There have been no access problems to date. The situation has been helped by the careful consideration shown by visiting climbers. It is not recommended that the quarry is used by organised groups as this may only serve to jeopardise existing access arrangements. Would visitors please take all of their litter home with them.

LOCATION AND APPROACHES

The quarry lies four miles to the north-west of Oswestry. Approach can be made by following the B4580 west of Oswestry town centre for two and a half miles. Turn right at the crest of the hill, opposite a post box, at a small signpost for 'Offas Dyke Path'. Follow this road for one mile to reach a T-junction with Carreg y Byg farm on the right. Turn right and then left almost immediately. Follow this road for some 500 yards, bearing left at a sign marked 'Tyn y Drain No through Road' and passing a farmhouse, to reach a gate and access track on the left. Park sensibly, taking care not to restrict access near the gate. Follow the track through the gate and the quarry lies down and on the left.

HISTORY

Climbing first began at Carreg y Byg in the late fifties when the quarry was discovered by local climbers Colin Perkins, Hadyn Morris and Bryan Phillips. Early routes included *Cave Arête* and *Little Girdle Traverse*. During the winter of 1960, they gardened some of the more obvious lines to produce further routes with *Cave Slab*, *Continuation Girdle*, *Steps* and *Perkins Route*. They were later joined by Paul Hill and development continued on a sporadic basis as more routes were cleaned and climbed. The classic *Forest Wall* dates from this period and was led by Bryan Phillips in 1962.

From approximately 1963 to 1967, another group of local climbers, namely Mike O'Gorman, Alan Samson, Simon Roddy and Charley Hardwick paid a number of visits to the quarry. The full extent of their activities during this period remains unclear, although their new routes certainly included *Freckled Hope* and *Mog*. Repeat ascents were also made of routes such as *Cave Arête*, *Continuation Girdle* and *Forest Wall Corner*.

After this initial activity development ceased and no further new routes were climbed until the eighties when more local climbers were made aware of the possibilities. Notably in 1981, Dave Barker led *Sundance Wall* and *Concave Wall*. In 1984 the quarry saw an unprecedented level of activity when a total of twelve new routes were climbed. Shrewsbury based climber Stuart Cathcart added *Physical Leverage* to the Forest Wall Area and another local, Adam Brown, contributed *Indecent Exposure* at the far end of the crag. Cathcart returned in 1985 to add further new routes with the appropriately named *Byg Arête* and *Byg Babies* on **Great Buttress**.

Further new routes were also climbed in 1986 and 1987, but following the publication of *Rock Climbs in the West Midlands* in 1988 there have been no further additions.

THE CLIMBS

Route lengths vary from 40ft to a maximum of 60ft and individual pitch lengths are not therefore included. Approach is made along the track from the gate and the quarry quickly comes into view down and on the left. A path leads down the steep bank to the quarry floor. The climbs are described from LEFT to RIGHT.

THE CAVE AREA

The first section of the quarry to come into view when approaching via the track. It has a pleasant and open aspect but unfortunately the rock is rather broken and featureless. There are a couple of small caves towards the left-hand side of the wall which help route identification.

1. **Cave Arête**   Difficult
    A direct line of ascent up the obvious arête to the left of the first small cave.

    a. **Little Girdle Traverse**   Severe, follows a traverse line from left to right beneath the upper bedding plane to finish up Cave Arête. Just to the right of Cave Arête, a steep path rises to the top of the crag.

CARREG Y BYG

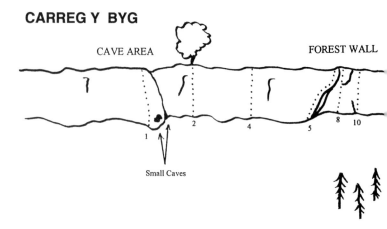

CAVE AREA

FOREST WALL

1

2

4

5

8

10

Small Caves

   b. **Continuation Girdle**,   Severe, starts from this path and traverses at two thirds height to finish up *Forest Wall Arête*.

2. **Cave Slab**   HVS 5A
   Start right of the small caves and climb the wall and slab directly to the large tree. Now much harder since several holds have fallen off.

3. **Cave Wall**   VS 4C
   Just right of *Cave Slab*, climb past the remains of a small tree to a crack on the arête and finish by trending right.

4. **Intermediate Arête**   Very Difficult
   This climbs the incipient arête below the thorn tree.

THE FOREST WALL AREA

This lies some 50 yards to the right past a number of minor possibilities. At the point where the access path becomes enclosed by trees there is a recessed wall. The next route starts just to the left of this recess.

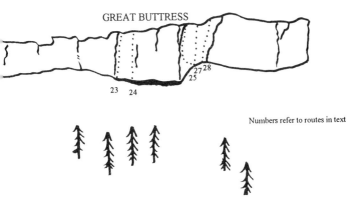

Numbers refer to routes in text

5. **Forest Wall Arête**   Very Difficult
    Climb the smooth slab moving rightwards to the arête. A
    few moves up this lead to a step right onto the upper
    headwall.

6. **Forest Wall Corner**   Very Difficult
    The obvious rightward-facing corner at the left-hand side
    of the recessed wall is climbed until a step left can be made
    to finish up *Forest Wall Arête* .

7. **Carreg y Byg Kid**   E2 5B
    Start just right of the corner and climb directly up the
    awkward bulging wall. Gain the short thin crack via an
    undercut and swing leftwards around the bulge to finish
    up *Forest Wall Arête*.

8. **Physical Leverage**   E2 5C **
    The central line of the recessed wall provides very good
    climbing. Start at the tree stump and climb directly up the
    steep wall to gain and finish up the thin crack in the
    headwall.

9. **Digital Sequence**   E1 5B *

Climb the short and dirty corner moving slightly leftwards to gain good holds in the wall above; bold. An awkward move up, peg runner on the right, leads to tricky moves up and then rightwards to finish.

10. **Forest Wall**   HVS 5B **

A local classic which serves as a good introduction to some of the harder routes in the quarry. Follow the leaning pillar and gain the slab above via the thin crack. Move up and left with difficulty, peg runner, and finish direct.

11. **New Wave**   E3 6A *

Climb directly up the initial mossy slab right of *Forest Wall* to pull over the bulge on poor holds. Finish right of the overhang as for *Rowan Route*. Unprotected.

Just to the right is;

12. **Rowan Route**   Hard Severe 4B

Struggle awkwardly past the trees to gain and climb the obvious crack. Well named!

13. **Dandelion Groove**   Hard Severe 4B

This climbs the shallow crack just right of *Rowan Route*, the exit being rather restricted by a large blackthorn bush.

14. **Ticket to Ride**   VS 4C

The thin crack 4 yards right of *Dandelion Groove* leads to a small overlap. Pull over this and finish rightwards up the vegetated slab, taking care with some suspect rock.

To the right is a large earth mound with a deep crack, *Fossil Crack*, rising directly above it,

15. **No Limits**   E3 5C

Start left of *Fossil Crack* and follow the short thin crack to pull directly over the overhang. Finish up the easier slab above.

16. **Fossil Crack**   VS 4C *

A good route following the obvious deep crack. Steep but well protected moves lead past the overhang at half height.

Finish more easily.

17. **Head Banger**   VS 4C
    The thin stepped crack just to the right of *Fossil Crack* has interesting climbing despite being rather vegetated.

18. **Freckled Hope**   VS 5A
    A direct line up the wall 5ft to the right of *Head Banger* leads to a loose finish up a shallow groove.

19. **Bruno Flake**   VS 4C
    This loose climb follows the steep wall to gain and climb the rounded arête just to the right of *Freckled Hope*.

The approach path now begins to descend as it approaches **Great Buttress**.

20. **Slip Slidin' Away**   Hard Severe 4B
    Dirty and overgrown. Climb the short, steep crack and then the slab above. Tricky for the grade.

21. **Prickle Finger**   VS 4B
    The undercut crack just right of *Slip Slidin' Away* and the dirty slab above.

22. **Part Time Study**   HVS 5A
    The short and technical corner forming the right-hand end of the slab is unfortunately very mossy.

Just to the right, **Steps,** Very Difficult, follows a line of steep rock steps leftwards through the vegetation. Surprisingly, this route sometimes ices up in winter and provides a pleasant Grade III climb.

GREAT BUTTRESS

The impressive front face of **Great Buttress** is severely undercut at its base. The first route starts at the left-hand side of this undercut.

23. **Fallen Birdman**   E1 5B *
    The undercut and recessed crack provides good climbing with a difficult and strenuous start leading to easier climbing on the mossy upper section. The initial difficulties are well protected.

24. **Tumbleweed**   E3 5C +
     An impressive route on dubious rock which would improve
     with further cleaning. Start just right of *Fallen Birdman*.
     Follow the thin crack through the undercut, peg runner on
     the lip, to gain the bulging wall above. This is followed
     leftwards, steeply to the top.

Around the arête to the right of *Tumbleweed*, the sidewall of
Great Buttress provides a further four routes.

25. **Byg Arête**   E4 6B ** +
     Start as for *Trepidation* but step left onto the very steep side
     wall and make a rising leftwards traverse on pockets and
     breaks to gain the arête beneath the overlap. Pull over this
     and finish direct with difficulty.

26. **Byg Babies**   E3 5C *
     Follow *Trepidation* into the niche. From the top of the niche,
     traverse 5ft left on a good break and pull up to gain a short
     overhang-capped groove. Follow this and pull strenuously
     over the overlap, moving right and then back left to a tree
     belay. Good climbing.

27. **Trepidation**   E2 5C **
     The route of the wall which provides excellent, steep
     climbing. Follow the stepped groove, cautiously, to the
     niche and good runners. Step right and finish in a superb
     position up the thin, technical crack in the headwall.

28. **Silver Girl**   E1 5B
     The least attractive of the routes hereabouts. Climb through
     the swastika overhangs right of *Trepidation* to gain a ledge.
     Follow the overhanging pod to the top. Some care is needed
     with loose rock.

Some 20 yards to the right of *Silver Girl*, **Crappy Crack** VS 4C
follows a scrappy crack line though a vegetated bay, yuck! A
further 10 yards to the right is a steep and loose arête with a
slender rightward facing wall to its right.

TREPIDATION Carreg y Byg
Climber: Paul Harrison Photo: Doug Kerr

29. **Mog**   E1 5B
    This climbs the steep crack line just to the right of the arête.
    There is a difficult problem start over the initial undercut
    and some care is required with the rock.

30. **Charlie's Aunt**   E4 5C
    This climbs the centre of the steep wall just to the right of
    Mog. A serious and strenuous route with the crux right at
    the top. The rock requires careful handling in places.

To the right, **Perkins Route**, Very Difficult, climbs the slabby
corner via the earth mound. This occasionally provides an ice
route during the winter. **Stagger**, Hard Severe 4A, climbs the
dirty staggered crack between *Perkins Route* and *Crystal Crack*.

THE SUNDANCE WALL AREA

The steep, clean wall some 15 yards right of *Perkins Route* offers
a concentration of good routes. The wall contains an obvious
straight crack, *Crystal Crack*.

31. **Barkers Route**   HVS 5B
    The steep wall 6ft to the left of *Crystal Crack* provides a
    difficult problem via a large pocket.

32. **Crystal Crack**   VS 4B   **
    The crack provides one of the most pleasant routes in the
    quarry. Steep and well protected climbing but some care is
    required on the finishing moves.

33. **Scoop Route**
    HVS 5A   *
    Good climbing. The wall just right
    of *Crystal Crack* passing a large
    thread. Finish direct.

34. **Sundance Wall**
    HVS 5A **
    A delightful route on impeccable
    rock. Climb the short finger crack
    before finishing direct or by
    moving left to join *Scoop Route*.

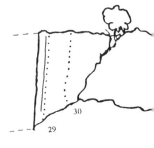

35. **Missing Link**   E3 5C *
Climb the wall just right of *Sundance Wall* with a hard move to gain good holds and small runners. Finish direct by fingery climbing.

36. **Concave Wall**   E1 5C **
The wall to the right is climbed past an in-situ thread runner with difficult, but well protected, fingery moves to gain the large tree.

37. **Indecent Exposure**   E2 5C **
The thin crack leads past a sloping ledge on the right. Finish directly up the short overhanging wall taking care on the final moves.

38. **Pakeha**   E1 5B *
A good traverse. Start as for *Stagger* and follow the obvious horizontal break to gain *Crystal Crack*. A tenuous line of small holds leads rightwards to the sloping ledge on *Indecent Exposure*. Follow this rightwards to finish.

Another traverse can be made of **The Sundance Wall** area at a much lower level, this is **The Stocking Top**, Severe.

CARREG Y BYG - Sundance Wall Area

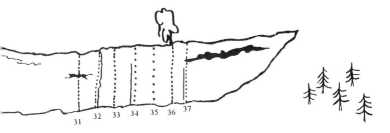

Numbers refer to routes in text

25

CARREG Y BYG: FIRST ASCENTS

Cave Arête	C.Perkins, H.Morris, B.Phillips, 1959
Little Girdle Traverse	C.Perkins, H.Morris, B.Phillips, 1959
Cave Slab	C.Perkins, B.Phillips, 1960
Continuation Girdle	C.Perkins, B.Phillips, 1960
Steps	B.Phillips, 1960
Perkins Route	C.Perkins (solo), 1960
Intermediate Arête	P.Hill, C.Perkins, B.Phillips, 1961
Forest Wall Arête	B.Phillips, C.Perkins, P.Hill, 1961
Forest Wall Corner	P.Hill, B.Phillips, C.Perkins, 1961
Forest Wall	B.Phillips, C.Perkins, April 1962
	A local classic.
Fossil Crack	C.Perkins, B.Phillips, April 1962
Crystal Crack	B.Phillips, C.Perkins, April 1962
	Another good discovery.
Rowan Route	B.Phillips, C.Perkins, April 1962
Dandelion Groove	P.Hill, C.Perkins, B.Phillips, 1962
Trepidation	B.Phillips, C.Perkins, 1962
	Two points of aid were used.
	First Free Ascent unknown.
Freckled Hope	A.Samson, C.Hardwick, 1965
Mog	M.O'Gorman, C.Hardwick, S.Roddy, A.Samson, 24/12/66. One peg for aid. First Free Ascent S.Cathcart, D.Barker, B.Phillips, 11/6/84
Barkers Route	D.Barker, B.Phillips, 4/5/81
Scoop Route	B.Phillips, D.Barker, 4/5/81
Sundance Wall	D.Barker, B.Phillips, 4/5/81
Concave Wall	D.Barker, B.Phillips, 4/5/81
Pakeha	B.Phillips, D.Barker, 4/5/81
	A good day!
Bruno Flake	B.Phillips, D.Barker, 17/5/82
Carreg y Byg Kid	M.Cameron, S.Cathcart, 12/5/84
Physical Leverage	S.Cathcart, B.Phillips, D.Barker, 13/5/84
Digital Sequence	B.Phillips, D.Barker, 13/5/84
Stagger	B.Phillips, S.Phillips, 13/5/84
Missing Link	B.Phillips, D.Barker, 13/5/84
Head Banger	A.Brown, B.Phillips, 3/6/84
Charlie's Aunt	S.Cathcart, C.Levington, 10/6/84
	A complete sandbag at the original grade of

HVS!

Silver Girl	B.Phillips, D.Barker, 12/9/84
	Two points of aid were used.
	First Free Ascent unknown.
Crappy Crack	B.Phillips, D.Barker, 12/9/84
Indecent Exposure	A.Brown, 1984
Fallen Bird Man	R.Hamer, A.Brown, 1984
Slip Slidin' Away	R.Hamer, A.Brown, 1984
Byg Arête	S.Cathcart, B.Phillips, D.Barker,29/4/85
	Aptly named.
Byg Babies	S.Cathcart, B.Phillips, D.Barker, 29/4/95
New Wave	D.Barker, B.Phillips, 17/5/85
Pricklefinger	B.Phillips, S.Phillips, 26/5/85
Part Time Study	B.Phillips, P.Phillips, 26/5/85
Ticket to Ride	K.Braddock, July 1986
Cave Wall	R.Jones, P.Abram, 1987
No Limits	R.Jones (solo), 1987
Tumbleweed	P.Roberts, A.N.Other. Date not known.

Publication of Rock Climbs in the West Midlands. 1988

CARREG Y BYG GRADED LIST

Byg Arête	E4	6B
Charlie's Aunt	E4	5C
New Wave	E3	6A
Byg Babies	E3	5C
No Limits	E3	5C
Missing Link	E3	5C
Trepidation	E2	5C
Physical Leverage	E2	5C
Indecent Exposure	E2	5C
Carreg y Byg Kid	E2	5B
Digital Sequence	E1	5B
Silver Girl	E1	5B
Concave Wall	E1	5C
Fallen Birdman	E1	5B
Barkers Route	HVS	5B
Forest Wall	HVS	5B
Scoop Route	HVS	5A
Sundance Wall	HVS	5A
Head Banger	VS	4C
Fossil Crack	VS	4C
Crystal Crack	VS	4B
Rowan Route	Hard Severe	4B
Forest Wall Corner	Very Difficult	
Forest Wall Arête	Very Difficult	
Perkins Route	Difficult	
Cave Arête	Difficult	

LLANYMYNECH QUARRY

by Gary Gibson

OS Ref: 265218   Sheet 126 (1:50,000 Landranger Series)

"This guide, though excellent and well produced of its sort is long overdue. That isn't a criticism of the authors, but of the amazing lack of interest that has been shown in the mile and a half of 100 to 150 foot high crags near to the road to Wales from the Midlands and the South. Perhaps now it's out, the faint hearted and those who didn't know it was there will take a trip to this crag which has everything......"

Review of Wolverhampton CC Guide. Rocksport April 1973.

APPROACHES AND SITUATION

Llanymynech Quarry is clearly visible overlooking the A483, the Oswestry to Welshpool road, on the southern outskirts of the village of Pant, some six miles from Oswestry. The Quarry is a prominent gash in the hillside which can be seen from miles around.

On the southern, Welshpool, side of Pant, a small crossroads will be found with a narrow, twisting road leading off to the right, seen when travelling from Oswestry. This road is not easy to locate, but is most easily identified by a 'gritstone-like' cottage and a row of 'tennis-racket-like' bollards on its southern corner. After two sharp bends, a dirt track ends in a very convenient parking area. From here, a good quarry-track leads to the cliffs.

CHARACTER

The rock in this quarry was once described as "comic" limestone by one of the local pundits, but whilst sarcastic in tone, this comment could be paradoxically thought of as relevant. Many of the older routes, due to the adventurous nature of the first ascensionists, take lines over vegetated and loose ground; all the routes were climbed on-sight without any form of prior knowledge and, perhaps more importantly, no removal of loose

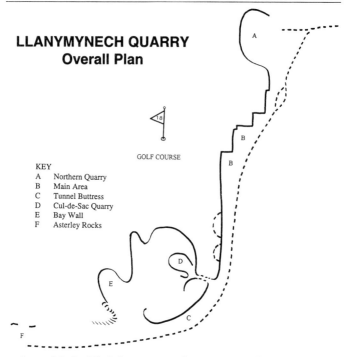

LLANYMYNECH QUARRY
Overall Plan

GOLF COURSE

KEY
A   Northern Quarry
B   Main Area
C   Tunnel Buttress
D   Cul-de-Sac Quarry
E   Bay Wall
F   Asterley Rocks

rock or debris. Had these routes become popular, then such a comment would have become redundant, but since such attitudes are now rather 'out-dated', the routes have become unpopular and un-trusted.

Modern methods have since been adopted and many of the harder routes, which subsequently take the cleaner and more imposing walls, have been well-gardened and breaks, cracks and holds have all been cleaned out. Modern methods of protection have also taken over and the majority of the routes, especially on **The Red Wall**, have in-situ gear adorning them. This has made the quarry much more wholesome in character and its routes far more appealing, although nowhere is the quarry over-burdened with ironmongery.

In recent years the quarry has suffered from a lack of attention on the easier lines. For this reason the less popular routes are becoming even less appealing and it was decided to reduce their description in the text. Only the more aesthetic have been described in detail. For those still wishing to sample the adventures take a full rack of gear, including pegs, hammer, helmet and faith in God, for the ultimate challenge.

PLEASE REFER TO THE DETAILED NOTES ON ACCESS BEFORE ATTEMPTING ANY CLIMBS.

On other sections of the quarry, the rock hides significant advantages. **The Red Wall** takes no seepage and is a welcome sun trap in winter. The wall and its more immediate neighbours also catch any early morning sunshine. On **The Red Wall** a little dust may be found on the more unpopular routes and, similarly on **The Black Wall**, some ledges do have sections of glutinous mud after a damp spell.

Overall, this is a very pleasant climbing ground. The flora and fauna give an added attraction in Spring and the routes described fully are of a very worthwhile nature. The cliff is rarely over-populated by modern-day standards and many of the locals out walking their dog or otherwise are of a very friendly nature. Please keep it that way.

ACCESS

Llanymynech Quarry is a nature reserve which contains an abundance of wildlife, especially rare plants and butterflies. The quarry is owned by Redland Aggregates Limited. The quarry is designated as a Site of Special Scientific Interest and is also an ancient monument of national importance.

Shropshire and Montgomeryshire Wildlife Trusts supported by English Nature and The Countryside Council for Wales share responsibility for looking after the site and its special features. In conjunction with the above bodies, The British Mountaineering Council have formulated the following access agreement, which must be adhered to in order for climbing to continue;

1) **NO ROCK CLIMBING MAY TAKE PLACE TO THE RIGHT OF CLEMATIS IN THE NORTHERN QUARRY.**

2) **NO ROCK CLIMBING MAY TAKE PLACE ON ASTERLEY ROCKS.**

3) Organised groups wishing to use **Cul-de-Sac Quarry** must first contact Peter Jones at the Red Ridge Centre, telephone 01938 810821, in order to prevent overcrowding.

4) Please help to conserve the plants and wildlife on the site by not leaving any litter or by removing or by disturbing soil or vegetation. There are many rare plants along the bottom of the quarry. Please take care when approaching the foot of the routes.

5) Clean only the existing routes, should this prove necessary. Further new route activity may result in the current access arrangements being withdrawn from parts or the whole of the quarry. Please note that unauthorised disturbance of plants or wildlife is a criminal offence under The Wildlife and Countryside Act 1981.

6) Birds of prey are currently nesting in **The Northern Quarry**. **In order to protect the birds, there is a breeding season ban on climbing on The Black Wall and The Red Wall from 1st March to 30th June.** Please check with the B.M.C. for any alteration to these dates.

7) Access to the site is to be strictly via the public rights of way.

8) Dogs must at all times be kept on leads.

9) The lighting of fires and the use of motor bikes are not allowed under any circumstances. Pushbikes may only be used on the bridle paths.

Much of the above is common sense. It has taken many hours of patient negotiations to secure access for climbers to enjoy the unique atmosphere of Llanymynech Quarry. Please do nothing

RAPTURE OF THE DEEP Llanymynech Quarry
Climber: Mike Owen Photo: Gary Gibson

to spoil or disrupt other peoples enjoyment of the site.

In an attempt to provide a full and accurate historical record, details of all climbs have been recorded in the text. Climbers are therefore requested to observe the access agreement outlined above and not to climb any routes in the Northern Quarry or on Asterley Rocks. All routes which are not covered by the present access agreement are therefore denoted with **(R), RESTRICTED,** and should be avoided. **THE INCLUSION OF THESE ROUTES IN NO WAY IMPLIES THAT CLIMBERS HAVE A RIGHT TO CLIMB THEM.**

HISTORY

Local children may justifiably lay claim to the first ascents of many of the easier routes at Llanymynech and even occasionally very swift descents. However, the true development of the quarry did not start until the mid sixties, when many of the easier routes in **The Main Area** were climbed by combinations of Peter and Malcolm Bayliss with Tony Booth. *Black Wall*, then known as *Black Slab*, was pegged into submission by Booth and D.Mitchell. This was free climbed some time later by Gordon Caine and Eddie Austrums at a rather undergraded Hard Very Severe.

In 1969, members of the Ceunant Club of Birmingham concentrated on the development of the quarry for some six months. Each team concentrated on specific areas of the quarry. Consequently, the names of R.Bennett, J.Brennan, M.Peacock, D.Irons and D.Sheldon featured prominently in the interim guidebook produced by Roger Bennett in 1970. The classic *Blind Faith* was climbed at this time.

The interest shown by the Ceunant Club precipitated the Wolverhampton Climbing Club, led by Gordon Caine, to attempt to work out the quarry in 1970. After a few days of familiarisation with the quarry, the routes started to fall rapidly, and in more ways than one! They began with *Kake* and the previously cleaned

BLACK IS BEAUTIFUL Llanymynech Quarry
Climber: Gary Gibson Photo: John Holdcroft/Gibson collection

Constrictor and swiftly followed up with the excellent *Cream* and *Zepplin*. The quarry also received its first extreme in the form of the long and steep *Power Game*.

After this frantic pace of development the quarry lay severely neglected during the latter part of the seventies. Indeed, only one further route was added in 1978, and the continued development did not resume until the mid 1980's.

Tales of huge, unclimbed limestone cliffs lured Peak District climbers to the quarry and consequently several hard and high quality routes followed. John Codling visited and was responsible for *Grid Iron*. A little later, Nick Dixon and Ian Dunn added two routes to **The Black Wall** with *Churnet Runners* (Dixon) and *While the Cat's Away* (Dunn). Doug Kerr then climbed the counter line to *Black Wall* and plugged an obvious gap with the appropriately named *Black is Beautiful*.

A little later, Kerr began the task of compiling a new guidebook to the area and with local climber Adam Brown began charting the quarry. This was to be the first easily available guide for around 15 years. As the guidebook went to press Nick Dixon moved into the area and with some spare time on his hands put his wealth of talent to good use on the huge unclimbed wall alongside *Power Game*. A superb wall climb and a quarried version of Lord of the Flies was produced with the outstanding *Nomad*. Dixon also managed the first breach of the overhanging Cul-de-Sac wall with *Spotty Dog*.

All was revealed in the guidebook and this huge quarry with large, unbreached walls, lay open to numerous possibilities for the climber with plenty of spare time on his hands.

One such climber was available in 1989 in the form of Gary Gibson who also had the time whilst recovering from a nasty accident. Gibson set about ravaging the quarry with a number of very worthwhile routes. **The Red Wall** was blitzed by a series of bolt routes, particularly meritable being The *Ancient Mariner* and *Mussel-Bound*. Gibson then moved over to 'work-out' the **Grid Iron Wall** with the classic being *Pew, Pew, Barney McGrew etc.* and also added immaculate companion routes to either side of *Nomad*. John Codling also returned to add a couple of new routes. As interest waned Gibson finished off his bout of activity with the desperate *Bill and Ben*, in name an antithesis of the route.

And so the quarry became more readily available to the climber with its cleaner and more imposing walls festooned with numerous routes. In the following years Gibson returned sporadically and eventually free climbed the old aided line in **The Northern Quarry** to end the latest chapter in the cliff's history. The route, *Too Many Teardrops*, provided a superb and fitting climax to this latest phase of development.

THE NORTHERN QUARRY **(R)**

This is the semi-circular quarry at the extreme right-hand end of **The Main Area,** most recognisable by dense ivy growth and being first viewed on the approach from the parking area. A direct approach, via one of the warren of tracks, leads through the jungle to the cliffs. The walls here are generally steep but cloaked in vast amounts of ivy. Unfortunately, two routes from the 1970's, **Vortex**, 210ft Hard Very Severe, **(R)** and **Bovarism**, 200ft E2 5C, **(R)** have since been engulfed by this vegatation and are now unidentifiable. A few routes, however, are easily found due to their present cleanliness.

In the extreme right-hand corner of the quarry there is a very impressive circular recess presenting the longest and most awesome single pitch in the quarry. Unfortunately, in the winter months, a pool often forms at its foot preventing direct access, unless of course a boat or icy conditions are available!

1. **Too Many Teardrops**   150ft E6 6B (7B+)   *** **(R)**
   A stunning route taking the central line of the huge hanging recess. Further description proves superfluous; follow the obvious line of 14 bolt runners, a small RP being useful before the first. Abseil off from a bolt belay below the crumbling capping overhang.

80 yards to the left of the recess, a clearing in the ivy provides one excellent route.

2. **Tropical Agent**   75ft E4 6A (6C+) ** (R)

    The obvious line of 7 bolt runners up the left-most side of the clearing gives sustained wall climbing directly to a lower-off station. Good clean climbing, often dry in wet weather.

The quarry now begins to swing round to the left forming a bay in its left-hand corner. The arête overlooking this bay and the remainder of **The Northern Quarry** provides the next route.

3. **Constrictor**   155ft Hard Very Severe **(R)** +

    Start just to the left of the arête at a clearing in the ivy.

    1. 110 feet. 5b. Climb up for 10ft and then traverse rightwards, peg runner at 40ft, to gain a niche. Move up and then rightwards, peg runner in a groove, but step left, climb up and back rightwards to enter the groove at a higher level. Follow this to ledges and then climb rightwards onto the arête which leads to a peg belay.

    2. 45 feet. Step left, move up and then back rightwards before climbing directly up to a tree belay.

To the left, an area of flat wall, again veneered in ivy, stretches out towards the daylight before terminating in a clean arête.

THE MAIN AREA

The most open section of the quarry which stretches from the obvious arête forming the right edge of **The Red Wall** to the sealed off tunnel driven through the left-hand end of the cliff.

THE RED WALL

The first area of clean rock encountered when approaching via the large track from the parking area. It has a characteristic, dusky red/orange appearance.

The climbing on this wall proves to be more of the sustained variety than the overly technical, save of course for the odd move. The majority of protection is fixed; these are very substantial bolts despite their unnerving appearance. Other useful protection points are described in the text. A word of

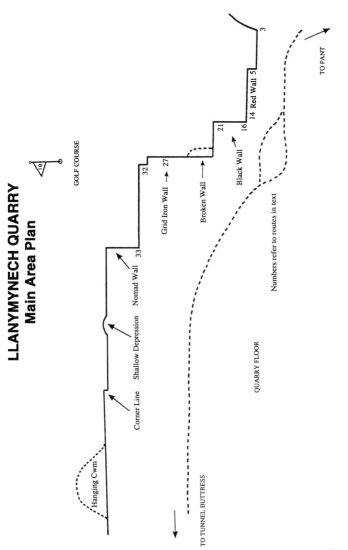

LLANYMYNECH QUARRY
Main Area Plan

GOLF COURSE

Hanging Cwm

Corner Line

Shallow Depression

Nomad Wall   33

Grid Iron Wall → 27   32

Broken Wall →

Black Wall →   21   16

14 Red Wall 5

3

TO PANT

Numbers refer to routes in text

QUARRY FLOOR

TO TUNNEL BUTTRESS

warning; some climbs are a little runout, calling more for the unerring leader than the frantic dash and grab brigade.

The wall is bounded on the right by a slim, soaring corner and to the left by a prominent arête, itself defining the edge of **The Black Wall**.

Note that climbing on **The Red Wall** is subject to **Annual Nesting Restrictions;** please refer to the detailed access notes before climbing here.

4. **Poison Ivy**   100ft E4 6A, 6B * (R)
   The slender right wall of the corner gives a good wall climb which is best split into two pitches.
   1. 50 feet. Tackle the centre of the lower wall via an obvious thin crack, numerous horizontal breaks and the occasional tortuous reach. Small wires and Friends prove essential. Belay at the first small ledge, bolt belay.
   2. 50 feet. The narrower, upper face is again taken centrally, preferably without using the arête (6A with). Three bolts and a good Rock 5 make protection more readily available. Abseil from a two bolt belay.

5. **Clematis**   100ft E4 5C, 5B
   The slim, soaring corner, whilst an impressive line, proves somewhat dirty and in need of a good clean.
   1. 50 feet. The lower section of the corner provides a hostile affair due to its dusty nature and lack of sound protection. Belay at a small ledge with a bolt belay on the right wall.
   2. 50 feet. Climb the upper corner via an excellent crack. Where it runs out, either use a two bolt belay on the right wall for retreat or battle through thorn bushes above to a muddy exit on the right; yuck! (90ft).

The upper reaches of **The Red Wall** have been breached by an incredible traverse along a series of wide and extremely dirty breaks. Whilst the route, **Space Odyssey,** 150ft Hard Very Severe, used four points of aid, it still stands as an awesome achievement and is yet to be repeated; go to it, but you'll need pegs as well as courage!

6. **Long John Codling**   100ft E4 6A (7A)   *
    The first route to the left of *Clematis* gives an exciting single pitch with a slightly unsound central section and strenuous upper reaches. High in the grade. Take a full rack to supplement the randomly placed in-situ protection. Climb the first slim groove 12ft to the left of *Clematis*, bolt runner, exiting rightwards onto some ledges. Continue gingerly up the wall above, peg runner, to reach a reasonable resting place as the wall rears up, peg runner. A series of difficult moves lead up this past a peg runner and a welcome bolt, to a prominent flake. Further tricky moves, bolt, lead up and then left to a two bolt belay. Abseil off.

7. **Mussel-Bound**   100ft E5 6A (7A+)   ***
    A superb pitch combining fingery, open climbing with sustained technical interest. The route of the wall. Start below the slim groove left of *Long John Codling.* Climb the left wall of the groove until, after 25ft, moves lead across onto its right-hand arête, Rock 1. Now pursue a direct line up the wall past a small corner and three bolt runners to a sharp borehole and the fourth bolt runner. The remaining 30ft are overhanging, have a fifth bolt, a downward pointing spike and a draining final reach. Abseil off from the two bolt belay above.

8. **Ship Dip**   100ft E4 6A (6C+)   *
    A worthwhile route with an enjoyable upper groove. Start 25ft left of *Mussel-Bound* at a higher level and just left of an elder tree. Climb the featureless wall trending slightly rightwards past three bolt runners to a shallow niche under a bulge, bolt runner. The bulge provides a difficult entry to a slim groove, bolt runner, which in turn leads to excellent holds and the final bolt. Traverse right to a two bolt belay and abseil off.

9. **The Deep**   85ft E4 6A (6C)   *
    The easiest route on the wall maybe, but still worthy of respect. Start 10ft left again below some narrow ledges low down on the wall. Pick a direct line up the wall past two bolt

runners and a perfect Rock 2 placement to reach a clean hanging slab, bolt runner. Pull onto this for a good rest, before moving left, bolt runner, and up via a ramp to a shaly break, bolt runner. A tricky move and wall lead to a two bolt belay. A 50m rope just reaches the ground when lowering.

10. **The Ancient Mariner**   130ft E5 6B (7A+)   ***
Atmospheric, absorbing and direct, the central line of the wall gains the top in one pitch; magnificent! Start in the centre of the wall at an arrow scratched in the rock. Move up to some small ledges, Rock 7 in a borehole, then move right and up through a tiny overlap, bolt runner, onto the wall proper. Go straight up this, bolt runner, to some rounded ledges, bolt runner, then step left and up to a bridged rest, peg runner. Extending moves lead rightwards to a hanging rib, bolt runner, where the technical crux ensues, bolt runner, to gain some good ledges, hidden peg in a corner to the left. Go straight up to gain the headwall, bolt runner, where bold climbing leads almost to the top. Move leftwards past a peg runner to twin trees and belay. Either battle through these or, better, abseil off.

11. **Dead Man's Fingers**   85ft E4 6A (7A)   **
An exciting and sustained route saving its hardest until last. 8 bolt runners show the way. From 15ft up *The Ancient Mariner*, move up and left to gain a small groove. Continue by taking a direct line, passing an overhang to the left, to reach a scoop. Exit directly, via a hanging rib, then move left to a two bolt belay.

The next trio of routes start from an ivy-coated platform below an overhang, 20ft from the left arête of the wall.

12. **Subterranean Sidewalk**   75ft E4 6A (6C+)   **
Probably the best introduction to the wall with straightforward though bold climbing after a hard start. Climb the arête springing from the right side of the platform, arrow, with a thin move past the first bolt to gain a small ledge. Continue up the steep wall above, two bolt runners,

to gain the right-hand side of a hanging slab and then a sharp ledge to its right, bolt runner. Follow the obvious vague rib above past a further bolt runner and a final unnerving pull to gain a two bolt belay directly.

13. **Rapture of the Deep**   80ft E5 6A (7A)   **

A fine companion route to *Subterranean Sidewalk* giving similar but slightly more technical climbing throughout. Climb up to the overhang and surmount it, bolt runner, to gain a wall and short arête, bolt runner. This leads up the centre of the hanging slab, peg runner. Stand up and step right to a bolt runner, from where a series of hard moves lead straight up to a shaly break, bolt runner. Move up a slim groove for 10ft, bolt runner, before gaining the two bolt belay on the right.

14. **Lobster on the Loose**   75ft E4 6B (7A)   *

A route characterised by an unusual and technical sequence at half height providing the hardest move on the wall. Climb the wall 10ft to the left of *Rapture of the Deep*, past a nose-grinding mantelshelf, bolt runner, to a standing position in a scoop, Friend 2. Move up and left to a good flake, Rock 5, then move up and back rightwards past a bolt runner to the foot of a ramp, bolt runner. The technical sequence ensues over the bulge, bolt runner, to a shaly break, bolt runner. Finish direct to a bolt and peg belay.

15. **Crab Stick**   75ft E4 6A (6C+)

The least inspiring route on the wall, but with plenty of exciting moments. Start 10ft right of the arête. Climb the wall, bolt runner, past a shattered area, Friend 3, to a second bolt runner on the fringe of the wall. Move up and slightly right to an undercut flake, bolt runner, and pull out right to a shaly break. Finish rightwards to a bolt and peg belay.

THE BLACK WALL

This is very obvious by name, its arête being formed by the junction of **The Red Wall**. The climbing here is characterised more by the technical, off-vertical variety than that of its more strenuous and immediate neighbour; an excellent contrast of styles.

At the time of writing the routes are in a good, clean state except for a few dirty ledges and the odd mud-filled break which are all on the easier sections of the routes. There is also a two bolt belay above the centre of the wall to enable a quick and easy means of descent.

Below the centre of the wall, a small, worn mound provides an obvious landmark for the start of several routes.

Please note that climbing on **The Black Wall** is subject to **Annual Nesting Restrictions;** please refer to the detailed access notes before climbing here.

16. **Zepplin**   120ft E2 5B

A worthwhile lower section is spoilt by a poor finish. The route takes the exposed arête at the junction of the Red and Black walls. Climb the slightly dusty lower wall on good holds, peg runner, past a borehole to reach the foot of an obvious shallow groove, peg runner. An excellent few moves up this lead to a step left onto the right edge of the black face. Now continue direct over poorer ground, past a third peg runner, moving left to gain the thin finishing crack of *Churnet Runners*.

17. **Churnet Runners**   120ft E4 6A   *

A pleasant route meandering up the right-hand side of the face. The difficulties are short-lived but two nails and two poor peg runners do not inspire confidence. Ascend easily up the right-hand side of the wall, minimal protection, to gain a thin break with a nail and an embedded, home-made piece of metal. Stand up and gain a real peg, not embedded! A quick technical pull leads to a small ledge, from where easier climbing leads up the face, peg runner, via some dirty ledges to a thin crack. Follow this to the top and belay off to the left.

LLANYMYNECH QUARRY
Black Wall

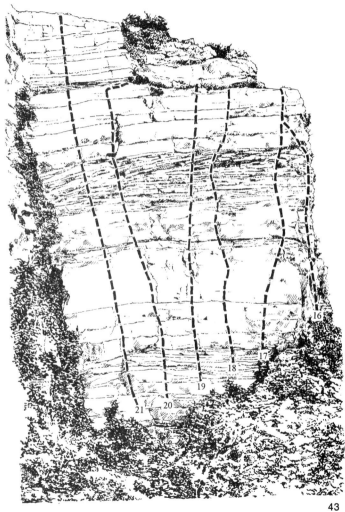

18. **Black is Beautiful**   120ft E4 6B   ***
    A direct, intricate pitch with one very hard but well protected move; the remainder feels reasonably bold. A superb and well-balanced blend, the most satisfying on the wall. Start from the foot of the mound. Take a direct line past a silver peg runner, the right-hand of two, to gain a prominent thin break dividing the wall. Carefully stand up and make a massive reach or hideous pull, bolt runner, to attain large holds. Step left and continue via a faint crack to easier ground. The finish lies above via a thin crack.

The next two routes have been re-described to give them a more logical directness. However, the starts and finishes can be easily interchanged by an interesting foot-traverse, either leftwards or rightwards, along the wide horizontal break at half-height. There is also an easier start to both routes on the left via a shallow groove and break from the top of the mound.

19. **Black Wall**   120ft E2 5B   ***
    An excellent route with pleasantly sustained climbing throughout. Protection is trustworthy though rarely plentiful. Start on the right-hand side of the mound. Pull over a tiny overlap and ascend via a faint crack, between two silver pegs, to gain the prominent deep pockets in the centre of the wall. Good holds in these, thread runner, lead to the wide horizontal break, from which a few wobbly moves lead up the thin crack, peg runner. From easy ground above press on directly to finish awkwardly up a short thin crack in the centre of the upper wall.

20. **Black Bastard**   120ft E2 5C   **
    The thin crack to the left of *Black Wall* provides a route similar in character, although it is technically harder for one move. From just below the top of the mound go straight up the face, peg runner, to gain the prominent thin crack. Stand up and make an unnerving move to gain the wide break. From here, slightly easier climbing, peg runner, leads to the base of the hanging corner. Climb this and then make an awkward rightwards traverse onto the grass terrace.

WHILE THE CAT'S AWAY Llanymynech Quarry
Climber: Unknown Photo: Gary Gibson

21. **While the Cat's Away**   130ft E4 6A   **

Another fine route completing the main quartet of the wall.
A short, technical section is combined with good moves
above and below. From the top of the mound, trend
leftwards up an easy groove and short wall to a break, peg
runner. The crux lies above, followed by another break,
peg runner, and a short wall leading to a ledge. Continue
left of a groove, Friends, up the short headwall. Tree belays.

22. **Picking Blackheads**   130ft E4 5C   *

The final route on the wall, squeezed in between *While the
Cat's Away* and the large vegetated corner. Very similar in
character to its neighbour but much bolder; worthwhile.
From 15ft up *While the Cat's Away*, move left to a sandy
alcove, (starting direct increases the grade to E5 without
side runners). Now go straight up the face just right of the
corner, sustained more than over-technical, wire protection,
to the obvious ledge system. The headwall is now taken
centrally, Friends, past a hole to the top.

The extremely over-grown corner dividing **The Black Wall**
from the wall on the left is taken by **The Old Fashioned Crab**,
160ft Very Severe. The centre of the wall, moving leftwards to
gain the arête is **Ivy Wall**, 150ft Severe and appropriately
named. The arête however is more worthwhile, whether taken
on its right or left-hand side and this can be gained via an easy
ledge system round to the left.

Around to the left of **Ivy Wall**, the wall is initially very broken
and disjointed. **Flake**, 110ft Hard Severe, takes a line up this wall
starting by a borehole, following an indefinite groove, passing
the left side of a triangular overhang and then finishing by
trending left to a crack. **Relaxative**, 150ft Very Difficult, moves
leftwards from the top of an earth mound and climbs the arête
of the smooth looking wall, or the dirtier groove to its right.
Odin's Beer Barrel Ramble, 175ft, Hard Very Severe, appears
by description to take a leftwards line across the smooth looking
wall to finish up a smooth groove at 5C; there are, however, no
signs of its peg runners on the wall.

PEW, PEW, BARNEY Etc. Etc. Llanymynech Quarry
Climber: Gary Gibson   Photo: Hazel Gibson

GRID IRON WALL

The large open wall to the left of the start of *Relaxative* is characterised by a long thin overlap at half height and a rather broken lower section. It then terminates on the left in a slim corner, separated from the main angle of the bay by a narrow, tapering wall.

The majority of the routes on this wall are well worth seeking out, with particularly fine upper sections. Take a full rack, including Friends 1-3.

At the bottom right-hand side of the wall, two vegetated terraces run into it from the right. From the left-hand end of the upper terrace springs;

23. **Humpty Dumpty**   130ft E4 6A
     Pleasant climbing squeezed onto the right-hand side of the upper wall. Climb straight up the relatively easy lower wall to gain a short, wide crack, usually with a plant sprouting from it. Move straight up to a ledge, then keep to the left of the upper arête on the excellent wall, two peg runners, to reach the big ledge 10ft from the top.

24. **Hickory Dickory Dock**   130ft E4 6A   *
     After a devious start the upper section of this route proves very attractive. Start at the bottom right-hand corner of the lower wall. Pick a line slightly rightwards via a niche, then move left to a ledge with an old peg, possible belay. The wall to the right leads to the halfway break, peg runner, trend right to gain the right-hand end of the overlap, peg runner, where technical moves gain another break. Enjoyable climbing leads leftwards via a thin crack to the final break where a traverse right gives an exit.

25. **Incy Wincy Spider**   130ft E5 6B   **
     A very substantial outing, high in the grade, incorporating a tough crux section with a bold feel to it. From the first ledge of *Hickory Dickory Dock*, belay advised, climb the thin crack to a break and ledge. Continue tentatively rightwards up the wall, peg runner, to the overlap, where a vicious

move, bolt runner, gains a resting place. Continue more easily up the headwall past a ring peg runner to the final break. Finish by moving left and then up.

26. **Pew, Pew, Barney, McGrew, Cuthbert, Dibble, Grub**
                            130ft E5 6B   **

The first of a trio of quality routes up the centre of the wall; very direct. Start below the middle of the grey wall below a borehole; arrow. Climb straight up via the borehole and a peg runner to a ledge. Move right to a right-facing corner and climb this and the extending wall above, peg runner, to the overlap. Power through, bolt runner, to a break, then carry straight on up to a faint finishing crack.

27. **Grid Iron**   130ft E4 6A   **

The original route of this expansive wall and in many ways its best. Open, varied and well protected climbing. From the ledge on *Pew, Pew etc*, move up the left-hand corner before swinging right into a thin crack. A few steep pulls lead to a resting place on the right. Continue slightly leftwards up the wall to finish via a sharp thin crack.

28. **Curfew**   130ft E4 5C   **

A superb wall climb, more sustained than hard and with an exciting finale. From the ledge on *Grid Iron*, move left across a broken ledge for 5ft. Continue up the wall via a series of breaks, peg runner, until moves slightly rightwards lead to a ledge. Move up to a bulge above and finish boldly up the leaning brown headwall above.

The upper wall to the left contains two routes, the lower parts of which are rather shattered. To gain the excellent upper sections either move left from *Curfew* for a one pitch route or abseil in and belay on the rope. The routes are described from the ledge.

29. **Gaza Strippers**   70ft E2 5C   *

The thin crack springing from the right-hand side of the ledge. The difficulties, low down past a poor peg runner, lead to well protected climbing above.

30. **A Night on The Town**   70ft E4 6A
     The wall between *Gaza Strippers* and the slim corner to the
     left provides a worthy companion. Finish via a thin crack at
     the top.

The appallingly vegetated corner to the left is taken by **Quasar**,
160ft, Hard Severe, which ventures onto the left wall at various
points as required.

   The next two routes take parallel lines on the lower half of the
aforementioned wall. Both retreat from a two bolt belay at 50ft.

31. **Smack the Juggler**   50ft E3 5C   *
     A nice warm up route which provides a sneak preview of
     the adjacent route. Climb the right-hand side of the wall via
     a thin groove and crack, peg runner, to a ledge. Move
     straight up, bolt runner, for 15ft before stretching left and
     up to the bolts.

32. **Jack the Smuggler**   50ft E4 6A (6C+)   **
     A miniature gem taking the centre of the wall. Bold above
     the first peg runner with technical moves above the next
     two. Move right and then up to the bolts.

The impressively vegetated main angle of the bay is **Disraeli
Gears**, 170ft, Hard Very Severe. The centre of the huge, featureless
wall provides two routes. **Quaker**, 150ft, Hard Very Severe,
climbs the middle of the wall via a wandering line and **The
Flying Mantuan**, 170ft, Very Severe, the left-hand side of the
wall by an undistinguished line and climbing! The arête bounding
the wall is **Broken Dreams**, 160ft Hard Very Severe, a broken
and disjointed route with some shattered rock and a peg for aid
below a crack on the top pitch.

   The huge slim wall to the left of the prominent arête provides
some of the most impressive climbing in the quarry; a trio of
routes with dramatic positions, superb rock and magnificent
wall climbing. All begin from the slender ledge at 40ft, gained
via the initial part of the arête.

33. **Unnamed**   120ft E3 6A   *
     The right-hand side of the lower wall and the left side of the

arête give a worthwhile pitch. Start just right of a bunch of
small trees on the ledge. The lower wall provides intricate,
technical climbing, peg runner, on small breaks to a wide
break and a friendlier area. Continue straight up the wall on
the left-hand side of the arête, always on good breaks,
Friend runners, and in a superb position. Exit on its right-
hand side to gain the top.

34. **This Won't Hurt**   120ft E5 6A   ***
An outstanding climb with brilliant wall climbing and airy
positions. Well cleaned and protected; take your Friends.
From behind the trees the initial wall gives fingery climbing,
bolt runner, until wider breaks give access to the right-hand
end of a long, narrow ledge. A technical move, bolt runner,
proceeded by more wide breaks, suprise, suprise, trending
slightly rightwards, lead to a sharp flake. Pull left and up
past a bolt runner to gain more breaks leading up to a deep,
thin break, peg runner. Balance right and finish up the left-
hand side of the arête, or, if you've plenty of spirit left, press
on direct at E6 6B.

35. **Nomad**   120ft E5 6A   ***
The central line of the wall and a suitable contender for 'the'
route of the quarry. Totally direct, thoroughly absorbing
and with sustained difficulties throughout. Climb the vague
groove 10ft left of the trees to a peg runner, then pull up
right to the long, narrow ledge. Continue up the wall above
to an overlap, peg runner, which is passed to the left via
breaks to a flake. A quick out-of-balance pull, peg runner,
gains a shaly break and respite. Continue up to a deep, thin
break, peg runner, and pull up right to a final peg. A series
of tricky moves above this constitute the crux and from a
wide break above, the wall eases for the top to be gained.

36. **The Screaming Skull**   120ft E5 6B   ***
In many ways the hardest route in this section of the quarry;
two difficult, technical sections are interspersed with the
sustained climbing typical of the wall. Immaculate. From

the long, narrow ledge on *Nomad*, move left and climb straight up the wall to just below a compact area of black rock, peg runner. A very technical balance move overcomes this and gains a resting place at a shaly break. The next section of the wall is more fingery, peg and two thread runners, and requires a long reach. Once gained, finish direct from the wide break.

The huge, unattractive corner to the left provides **The Nibbler**, 120ft, Very Severe, using both the right and left wall when necessary. **Power Game**, 120ft, E1 5B, is probably the best route on the wall to the left, taking a shallow groove system starting 10ft to the left of the corner, before finishing up a prcminent, overhanging crack.

The walls to the left now become extremely broken and vegetated for some 100 yards before a large 'hanging cwm' is reached. For the most part the routes here are characterised by poor climbing, loose rock and few noteworthy qualities. Hence, only brief descriptions are given.

Blood, Sweat and Tears, 205ft, Very Severe 4B, takes the broad, shallow depression starting a third of the way along the wall from *The Nibbler*. **Alphaville**, 190ft, Very Severe, takes a direct line up the wall between *Blood, Sweat and Tears* and the corner on the left-hand side of the wall. **Brave New World**, 180ft, Very Severe, takes the corner itself.

At the left-hand end of the wall, where it falls back into the 'hanging cwm', there is an arête with a leftward facing corner to its right. To the right of this arête a cone of soil ascends the wall for a few feet with a group of ivy coated blocks on the right; **Lurid Honk,** 160ft, Hard Severe, takes the loose walls above the blocks; **Insanity**, 180ft, Severe, takes the groove line that starts in the apex of the arête to the left of *Lurid Honk* and proves pleasant; **Treasure Trove**, 150ft, Severe, which certainly isn't, takes a line up the right-hand side of the hanging cwm and **Mr Magoo**, 200ft, Very Difficult, takes its left-hand side.

To the left of the hanging cwm, the obvious corner in the buttress gives **Debut**, 180ft, Very Severe, and **Bolg**, 60ft, Severe, takes a prominent crack running up the wall at the back of the second cwm.

To the left, the left retaining wall of the second cwm sports an overhanging crack giving the aid route **Stone the Crows**, 110ft, Hard Very Severe and A1. And finally in this section of the quarry, the loose looking red wall can be climbed via a diagonal line to give **Evil Woman**, 90ft, Severe.

TUNNEL BUTTRESS

This is the continuation of **The Main Area** beyond the entrance to the prominent, and now sealed-off, entrance to the massive through tunnel bored into the cliff. The rock here is short and steep with few natural lines and plenty of encroaching vegetation.

The Grooviest, 115ft, Hard Very Severe, follows an undistinguished groove 100 yards to the left of the tunnel entrance, starting below a crack and overhang. The remaining routes are concentrated in the left-hand section of the cliff before it turns a full 180 degrees into **The Cul-de-Sac Quarry.**

Starting 30 yards to the right of a fence and right of a huge ivy patch is; **Battered Ornaments**, 85ft, Hard Very Severe 1pt aid, which takes an overhang with a peg for aid and then a line above via a groove and slab to finish up loose rock. **Bolder**, 120ft, Hard Very Severe, 1pt aid, takes a line above an ivy-covered boulder just to the left with peg for aid to pull over a small overhang at 30ft. Directly from the fence ascends **Windy**, 110ft, Very Severe, via a rightwards line to a large block and then a direct finish.

At the extreme left-hand end of the buttress, the wall curves around to face **Blind Faith Buttress**. **Barad Dur**, 50ft, Severe, takes a loose, shallow groove, **Bring on the Nubiles**, 50ft, Very Severe, 4C, takes a line 20ft to the left and **Floating Roses**, 50ft, Severe, ascends a line just to the left of a man-made cave.

CUL-DE-SAC QUARRY

This is the small quarry which could once be reached by going through the tunnel. Instead, since its closure, continue round to the right and drop down an old, stony quarry ramp into its base alongside the tunnel entrance. Here will be seen an impressive, though short, overhanging wall with an obvious black wall opposite; a popular spot with organised groups.

The routes are described in an anti-clockwise direction around the quarry from RIGHT to LEFT.

37. **Andy Pandy** 30ft E4 5C
    The prominent, leaning arête on the right-hand side of the descent ramp, taken direct. Unprotected.

38. **Merde!** 50ft Hard Severe 4A
    The right-hand end of the obvious black wall is a popular line of descent by abseil. Dirty.

39. **Voila!** 50ft Difficult
    The leftward trending line of weakness and short groove. Finish direct from a block.

40. **Ca Va!** 50ft Very Difficult
    The broken crack on the left, finishing awkwardly from a niche.

41. **Eh Bien!** 50ft Very Difficult
    Pull into the bottomless groove forming the left-hand side of the wall, then climb leftwards to finish up the left side of a pink wall.

42. **Alors!** 50ft Difficult
    The loose and broken wall to the left of *Eh Bien!*

The walls now fall back into a broken bay with several short scrambles of little consequence. The main, overhanging wall provides more meaty pitches requiring plenty of gusto. Take your Friends.

43. **Saul's Crack** 35ft Very Severe 4C
    The short and steep crack on the right-hand side of the wall.

44. **Bill and Ben** 35ft E6 6C (7C) *
    Attack the wall 10ft left of *Saul's Crack* past a lonesome peg runner. This is the hardest route in the quarry which requires plenty of strength as well as an impressive dyno.

45. **Spotty Dog**   35ft E5 6B (7A+) *
    Start in a small, right-facing corner below the centre of the
    face. The corner and initial wall prove easy, the finish is not.
    Plenty of old in-situ gear and ironmongery provide comfort.

46. **Little Weed**   35ft E5 6B (7B)   **
    The thin crack system on the left-hand side of the wall
    provides its best route; fingery and strenuous with three
    bolt runners.

47. **Slobberlob**   35ft E4 6B   *
    Starting 5ft right of the arête, climb the leaning wall direct
    past a buried peg runner. 6A for the tall.

BLIND FAITH BUTTRESS

This is the buttress that lies to the left of the fenced-off plantation
in the upper quarry; an impressive buttress with a number of
worthwhile routes that trace weaving lines in-between its
overhangs. The routes are described from RIGHT to LEFT.

48. **Cream**   160ft Very Severe   *
    A good route up the right-hand arête of the buttress. Start
    at a point where the fence meets the rock.
    1.50ft. 4B. Climb steeply to a peg runner, then move up and
    right on undercuts to follow a crack to a ledge on the right
    with a large perched block. Peg belay.
    2.60ft. 5A. Move left onto a flake in a groove and thence to
    a small ledge. Traverse left to the arête and follow a short
    groove, then move left to belay in a shallow cave on the
    buttress front.
    3.50ft. 4A. Pull out of the cave and finish easily.

49. **Requiem**   175ft Very Severe (2pts aid)   +
    This route follows the right-hand arête of the front face of
    the buttress and finds a way through the prominent red
    caves. Start below a short crack to the right of a mass of ivy
    in the centre of the buttress.
    1. 35ft 4B. Follow the crack leftwards and pull round a
    jammed block. Move up to a stance in the first cave.

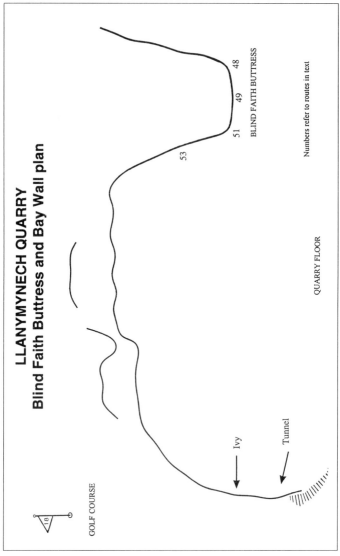

LLANYMYNECH QUARRY
Blind Faith Buttress and Bay Wall plan

BLIND FAITH BUTTRESS

Numbers refer to routes in text

QUARRY FLOOR

48
49
51
53

Ivy

Tunnel

GOLF COURSE

18

2. 45ft. 4B. Move left and climb the wall to the roof. Move left using two pegs for aid to a peg runner on the left. Swing up and left to good ledges and a belay on the highest of these in the second cave.

3. 95ft. 4C. Move up and left to a crack splitting the roof, then traverse leftwards onto the left wall, peg runner. Move back right to an undercut ledge, before finishing on superb holds.

50. **Strawberry Milkshake**   125ft Very Severe (1pt aid) +

1. 45ft. 4B. Climb the initial crack of *Requiem* and then continue up to the roof. Traverse right to a large stance and belay.

2. 20ft. 5A. Use a nut for aid to attain a standing position on the lip of the overhang. Move right and climb the small arête to ledges and a belay.

3. 60ft. 4B. Climb the steep wall above the belay with poor protection but good holds to the terrace. Easy ground leads to the top.

51. **Sentinel**   170ft Very Severe   +

This route finds a way up the left-hand arête of the buttress. On the front of the buttress there is a short wall with two grooves in its left-hand end. Start beneath the left-hand groove.

1. 80ft. 4C. Go up the short groove to the ledge and follow the easy groove above to the overhangs. Step left to a ledge and go up a steep wall to a perched block. Move left to a thin crack and follow it to a good stance on the arête.

2. 90ft. 5A. Move up and right to a peg runner at a borehole. Follow the wall trending leftwards to the top.

52. **Blind Faith**   150ft Very Severe   **

The obvious groove line on the left-hand side of the prow of the buttress. A good route with plenty of atmosphere. Start as for *Sentinel* below the left-hand groove.

1. 50ft 4B. Go up the short groove, then move left and climb the main groove in the slab to a large perched block. Step

left around the arête to a good stance below the main groove. This point can be gained direct via a crack which is reached from the left.

2. 40ft. 4B. Climb the groove to a peg belay below the overhang.

3. 60ft. 4B. Move up and left to a small ledge, step right and then go back left to a wall which leads to a final short wall. Pull up onto a block on the left and mantelshelf airily to the top. Scramble off to the left.

53. **The Grateful Dead**   145ft Hard Very Severe (1pt aid)+
This follows the shallow, leftward-trending groove line in the centre of the reddish wall, some 30ft to the left of *Blind Faith*.

1. 100ft. Follow the groove directly for 50ft to reach a peg runner where it steepens. From a friable ledge, move up to a bulge and pull over a shattered niche, bong for aid. Move up and left to a good ledge and peg belays.

2. 45ft. Move left, peg runner, and climb the wall to a large ledge, peg runner in the flake crack. Step left into a wide groove and follow it to the top.

It's a Beautiful Day, 270ft, Very Severe, 2pts aid, is a girdle traverse of the buttress from left to right, starting to the right of some ivy, at the right-hand end of the broken walls to the left. A poor route.

BAY WALL AREA

The semi-circular area of the quarry lying immediately to the left of **Blind Faith Buttress**. This is rather a featureless and broken area. From RIGHT to LEFT are;

Trepidation, 120ft, Severe, takes a leftwards line above some ivy, eventually finishing rightwards. **Spooky Tooth**, 140ft, Hard Severe, is a vague line above a shallow depression and whitish overhang. The blunt rib left again is **Bridge of Thighs**, 110ft Severe, and 10ft left again is the wandering **The Cowardly Deviant**, 110ft, Severe. A faint groove to the right gives **I.C.I. (Intergalactic Cottage Industries)**, 150ft, Very Severe.

To the left again a soil ramp marks the start of yet more routes. **In Absentia**, 110ft, Severe, follows a blunt rib pointing the way to poor rock above. **Pickled Mothball**, 120ft, Severe, follows a curving line of weakness to the left and **Pink Panther**, 130ft, Hard Severe, lies to the left again.

To the left at the back of the bay, a tunnel, sometimes obscured by a large tree, is an obvious landmark. The two ivy patches to the right are split by a very narrow clean streak: **Caramba**, 140ft, Very Severe. **Nenderthal**, 80ft, Hard Very Severe, takes a wandering line 15ft left of the tunnel and **Waterslide**, 80ft, Very Severe, climbs above some boreholes 5ft left again. Believe it or not, the whole area is girdled: **Bay Wall Girdle**, 240ft, Severe.

ASTERLEY ROCKS **(R)**

This is the continuation of the quarry some 200 yards beyond **Bay Wall Area**. Approach is made by the footpath which contours around the hillside. The first buttress reached has a low cave at its base and provides two very poor routes, **Swan Song**, 100ft, Very Difficult **(R)**, on the right and **Haystack**, 95ft, Very Difficult **(R)**, on the left.

Continuing leftwards along the path there is a smooth, thin wall which is set above broken ledges. This provides some pleasant climbing on good rock. From RIGHT to LEFT are:

54. **Grooved Prune** 60ft Very Difficult **(R)**
    This climbs the right-hand side of the smooth wall via a series of ledges.

Beginning from the grass terrace above the ledges are:

55. **Ding** 30ft Very Severe 5A **(R)**
    Gain and climb the shallow groove and pull directly through at its closure to finish up the wall above.

56. **Kalashnikov** 30ft Hard Very Severe 5B **(R)**
    From the shallow niche on Ding, traverse left for 6ft to finish straight up the wall above.

57. **Fore** 30ft Hard Very Severe 5A *** (R)**
    Just to the left a very shallow groove leads awkwardly onto

the upper wall. Step left and finish with a long reach.

58. **Margaret's Wall**   30ft Very Severe 4C   * **(R)**
The short wall leads onto the ledge. Continue direct following the thin, broken crack.

59. **Dong**   30ft Severe **(R)**
The shallow groove towards the left-hand end of the wall. Steep, but with 'enough good grips'.

The final route, **Paydirt**, 30ft, Very Difficult **(R)**, climbs the poor, loose wall left of the Margaret Asterley plaque.

LLANYMYNECH QUARRY FIRST ASCENTS
Compiled by Doug Kerr.

Details of the following routes are unknown; **Barad Dur, Volia!, Ca Va!, Eh Bein!, Alors!, Merde!**

Ivy Wall	A.Booth and Mrs P.Booth, 1966
Quasar	D.Mitchell and A.Booth, 1966
Grooved Prune	A.Booth, A.Padfield and R.Pinner, 1966
Black Slab	A.Booth and D.Mitchell.
	An aid route involving sections of both *Black Wall* and *Black Bastard*.
Treasure Trove	P.Bayliss, M.Bayliss and A.Booth, 1967
The Cowardly Deviant	P.Bayliss.
Blind Faith	M.J.Peacock and D.Irons, 22/11/69
	Direct start added by G. Caine, date not known.
	The discovery of a local classic.
Trepidation	R.Bennett, D.Sheldon and M.Cooke, (varied leads), 22/11/69
In Absentia	R.Bennett and J.Brennan (alternate leads), 29/11/69
Sentinel	M.J.Peacock and D.Irons, 30/11/69
Pickled Mothball	J.Brennan and R.Bennett (alternate leads), 27/12/69
1887 Rock Climbing Company	R.Bennett and J.Brennan (alternate leads), 1/1/70

Bridge of Thighs	J.Brennan and R.Bennett (alternate leads), 4/1/70
Requiem	M.J.Peacock and J.Brennan, 21/1/70
	Two points of aid were used.
Spooky Tooth	D.Irons and M.Perry, 25/1/70
Intergalactic Cottage Industries	R.Bennett and J.Brennan (alternate leads), 25/1/70
	Pitch two was later climbed direct by G.Caine, date not known.
Pink Panther	D.Sheldon and A.Dowell (alternate leads), 25/1/70
Haystack	P.Hay and R.Hay, 25/1/70
	A busy day at Llanymynech!
Broken Dreams	F.Cannings, P.Littlejohn and C.Morton, 31/1/70. One point of aid was used.
The Nibbler	D.Sheldon and D.Irons, 1/2/70
Clematis	R.Lavill and S.Jones, 7/2/70 Aid pitch. First free ascent unknown.
The Flying Mantuan	D.Irons and D.Sheldon, 8/2/70
Brave New World	D.Irons and D.Sheldon (alternate leads), 14/2/70
Insanity	R.Bennett and J.Brennan (alternate leads), 14/2/70
The Grateful Dead	M.J.Peacock and M.C.Cooke, 14/2/70
	One point of aid. Another busy day!
Blood, Sweat and Tears	D.Irons and D.Sheldon (alternate leads), 15/2/70. One point of aid.
Relaxative	M.Burgess and M.Cook, 21/2/70

Interim Guidebook to Rock Climbing at Llanymynech Crags. Edited by Roger Bennett.

Lurid Honk	J.Brennan and D.Sheldon (alternate leads), 15/3/70
Battered Ornaments	D.Irons and D.Sheldon, 5/4/70. One point of aid.
Alphaville	D.Irons, D.Sheldon and M.Cooke (varied leads), 19/4/70
Fake	G.Caine, G.Poole and D.Burton, 26/4/70
Constrictor	G.Caine and D.Wilkinson, Easter 1970
Space Odyssey	D.Irons and D.Sheldon, 1/5/70
	"To boldly go where no man has been before..." and to where no man has since returned!

	Four points of aid were used.
Knotted	G.Caine and D.Burton, 10/5/70
Debut	K.G.Hopkins and A.Houghton (alternate leads), 10/5/70
Cream	D.Cuthbertson and G.Caine, 23/5/70
Zepplin	G.Caine and D.Cuthbertson, 25/5/70 One point of aid. First free ascent S.Hardy, 1986
Caramba	G.Caine and G.Poole, 31/5/70
Saul's Crack	G.Caine and D.Cuthbertson, July 1970
Quaker	G.Caine and R.Hibbert, July 1970
Bay Wall Girdle	R.Bennett and J.Brennan, pitches 1 to 4 (alternate leads) R.Bennett and R.Hodgkinson pitch 4. Completed 19/7/70
Disraeli Gears	D.Irons and D.Sheldon (alternate leads), 19/7/70
Windy	G.Caine and R.Hibbert, 31/7/70
Power Game	G.Caine and R.Hibbert, 1/8/70
The Old Fashioned Crab	D.Sheldon and J.Brennan, 2/8/70
The Grooviest	G.Caine, D.Wilkinson and R.Hibbert, 9/8/70
Waterslide	R.Astley and P.G.Hall, 13/8/70
Bolg	D.Burton and M.Thompson, August 1970
It's A Beautiful Day	D.Irons and M.C.Cooke, 3/10/70. Two points of aid.
Stone the Crows	D.Irons and M.C.Cooke, 4/10/70. Aid pitch.
Vortex	M.Jones and K.Bowen, 4/10/70. Appropriately named as this route has now disappeared into the vortex!
Black Wall	G.Caine and E.Austrums, 4/10/70. This free climbed sections of the aid route Black Slab. The original description of Black Wall has been changed to provide a more logical and direct route. A direct start, as presently described, was added by D.Kerr and S.Grove on 25/7/87
Odin's Beer Barrel Ramble	M.Jones and S.Hogge, 18/10/70. One point of aid.
Evil Woman	D.Irons and P.Robbins, 24/10/70

Swan Song	J.Brennan and R.Bennett (alternate leads), 8/11/70
Mr Magoo	D.Irons and B.Webb, 14/2/71
Bolder	G.Caine and R.Hibbert, 23/5/71. One point of aid.
Fighting Roses	R.Thursfield and P.Morris, 25/6/71
Bovarism	E.Edkins and K.Argyle, June 1971. Three points of aid.
	First free ascent unknown.
Neanderthal	P.G.Hall and R.Astley. Date not known.
Echelon	P.Robbins and D.Irons. Date not known. Aid pitch.

Guidebook to Llanymynech Quarry published by Wolverhampton MC, edited by Roger Bennett and Gordon Caine, 1973.

Strawberry Milkshake	G.Bennett and M.Bartley, 1978. One point of aid.
Bring On The Nubiles	A.Brown. Date not known.
Grid Iron	J.Codling. Date not known.
Gaza Strippers	S.Hardy and A.Popp, 1986
While The Cat's Away	I.Dunn and N.Dixon, 1986
Churnet Runners	N.Dixon and S.Hardy, 1986
Black Bastard	D.Kerr and P.Stacey, 1/6/87. Climbed in a thunderstorm, hence the name!
Black Is Beautiful	D.Kerr (unseconded), 8/8/87
Dong	D.Kerr (Solo), 26/9/87
Margaret's Wall	D.Kerr and S.Grove, 26/9/87
Fore	D.Kerr (unseconded), 26/9/87
Ding	D.Kerr (unseconded), 26/9/87
Spotty Dog	N.Dixon and A.Popp, 1988
Nomad	N.Dixon and A.Brown, 1988

Rock Climbs in the West Midlands published 1988.

Kalashnikov	A.Brown and K.Jones, July 1988
Little Weed	G.Gibson (unseconded), 11/2/89. First free ascent of Echelon.
Hickory, Dickory, Dock	G.Gibson (unseconded), 11/2/89
Incy, Wincy Spider	G.Gibson (unseconded), 21/2/89
Curfew	G.Gibson (unseconded), 21/2/89
The Ancient Mariner	G.Gibson (unseconded), 4/3/89
Jack The Smuggler	G.Gibson (unseconded), 11/3/89
This Won't Hurt	G.Gibson (unseconded), 11/3/89. Climbed direct by G.Gibson, 23/8/89 (unseconded)
Humpty Dumpty	G.Gibson (unseconded), 14/3/89

Picking Blackheads	G.Gibson (unseconded), 15/4/89
Pew, Pew, Barney (etc)	G.Gibson (unseconded), 15/4/89
A Night On The Town	G.Gibson (unseconded), 15/4/89
Smack The Juggler	G.Gibson and H.Gibson, 15/4/89
	Another busy day!
Lobster On The Loose	G.Gibson (unseconded), 22/4/89
Rapture Of The Deep	G.Gibson (unseconded), 22/4/89
Subterranean Sidewalk	G.Gibson (unseconded), 22/4/89
Slobberlob	G.Gibson (unseconded), 22/4/89
Poison Ivy	G.Gibson (unseconded), 22/4/89
	An even busier day!
	The top section was climbed by G.Gibson (unseconded), 20/9/89
Dead Man's Fingers	G.Gibson (unseconded), 29/4/89
Crab Stick	G.Gibson (unseconded), 29/4/89
The Screaming Skull	G.Gibson (unseconded), 29/4/89
Bill and Ben	G.Gibson (unseconded), 29/4/89
Andy Pandy	G.Gibson (Solo), 29/4/89
Un-named	J.Codling and C.Calow, May 1989
Paydirt	D.McSorley and K.Toft, 22/6/89
Long John Codling	J.Codling and G.Gibson, 2/7/89
Ship Dip	G.Gibson and D.Kerr, 15/7/89
The Deep	G.Gibson and D.Kerr, 15/7/89
Mussel-Bound	G.Gibson (unseconded), 15/7/89
Too Many Teardrops	G.Gibson (unseconded), 3/11/90
Tropical Agent	G.Gibson, 7/3/92

THIS WON'T HURT Llanymynech Quarry
Climber: Gary Gibson Photo: John Holdcroft/Gibson Collection

LLANYMYNECH QUARRY: GRADED LIST

Bill and Ben	E6	6C	
Too Many Teardrops	E6	6B	
The Screaming Skull	E5	6B	
Incy Wincy Spider	E5	6B	
Little Weed	E5	6B	
Nomad	E5	6A	
The Ancient Mariner	E5	6B	
Mussel-Bound	E5	6A	
Spotty Dog	E5	6B	
This Won't Hurt	E5	6A	
Pew, Pew, Barney McGrew	E5	6B	
Rapture of the Deep	E5	6A	
Lobster on the Loose	E4	6B	
Long John Codling	E4	6A	
Black is Beautiful	E4	6B	
Hickory Dickory Dock	E4	6A	
Poison Ivy	E4	6A	6B
Dead Man's Fingers	E4	6A	
Crab Stick	E4	6A	
Grid Iron	E4	6A	
Ship Dip	E4	6A	
While the Cat's Away	E4	6A	
Tropical Agent	E4	6A	
A Night on the Town	E4	6A	
Subterranean Sidewalk	E4	6A	
Slobberlob	E4	6B	
Jack the Smuggler	E4	6A	
The Deep	E4	6A	
Curfew	E4	5C	
Picking Blackheads	E4	5C	
Churnet Runners	E4	6A	
Clematis	E4	5C	5B
Unnamed	E3	6A	
Smack the Juggler	E3	5C	
Gaza Strippers	E2	5C	
Black Bastard	E2	5C	
Black Wall	E2	5B	
Zepplin	E2	5B	

OAK TREE WALL DIRECT Pontesford Rocks
Climber: Doug Kerr Photo: Steve Adderley

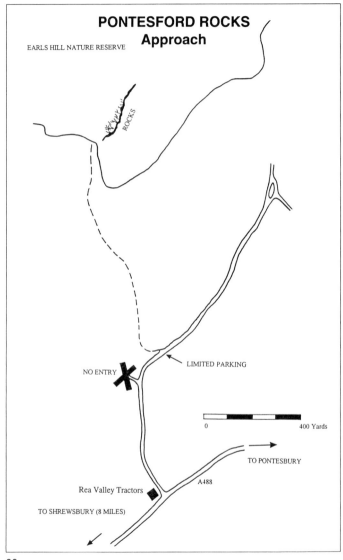

PONTESFORD ROCKS
Approach

EARLS HILL NATURE RESERVE

ROCKS

LIMITED PARKING

NO ENTRY

0   400 Yards

TO PONTESBURY

A488

Rea Valley Tractors

TO SHREWSBURY (8 MILES)

PONTESFORD ROCKS

OS Ref: 409047 Sheet 126 (1:50,000 Landranger Series)

"Although the crag, which lies on the south side of Pontesford Hill, cannot compete in severity with some of the well known gritstone outcrops, it nevertheless offers some fifty routes for the climbers' delight, some of which are two hundred feet long. Furthermore, it is the most important crag for many miles around, and certainly the nearest to the industrial centres of the West Midlands."

W. Unsworth 1962.

Please note that the current text has been edited considerably since this guidebook appeared in 1962.

SITUATION AND CHARACTER

Pontesford Rocks are delightfully situated some eight miles to the south-west of Shrewsbury on the south side of Earls Hill. The summit of Earls Hill provides superb views of the Shropshire Hills and is the site of an Iron Age fort.

The rock at Pontesford is pre-Cambrian Welsh igneous and is generally sound, although care should be exercised on some of the more obscure routes. Pontesford Rocks have been popular for over sixty years as a beginners' playground with a number of good quality low grade rock climbs with plentiful belays.

APPROACH

Pontesford Rocks are best approached from Shrewsbury via the A488, the Shrewsbury to Bishop's Castle road. When approaching from Shrewsbury, Earls Hill is seen as a very distinctive 'hump-backed' hill. On reaching the village of Pontesbury, turn left just after Rea Valley Tractors. Follow this lane for a quarter of a mile to reach a fenced off Forestry clearing marked 'Pontesford Hill' with some limited roadside parking just beyond. Follow the **lower** footpath, through the clearing, and around the base of the woods to cross a large field reaching a gate at the entrance to Earls Hill Nature Reserve. Pass though the gate and turn right to follow a path up the scree slope. The path rises quickly to pass through trees at **Fifty Foot Wall** and continues upwards passing behind **Pontesbury Needle** to gain a col beneath **The West Buttress**. The col provides a convenient base-camp and an opportunity to recover from the tortuous fifteen minute walk!

ACCESS

Pontesford Rocks form part of the Earls Hill Nature Reserve, a Site of Special Scientific Interest, managed by the Shropshire Trust for Nature Conservation. Whilst not wishing to prohibit climbing, the Trust is concerned that this should be properly regulated in order to preserve the reserve status of the rocks. CLIMBERS USING THE ROCKS SHOULD PAY DUE REGARD TO THE ECOLOGICAL INTERESTS OF THE SITE. CAMPING IS NOT PERMITTED.

HISTORY

Birmingham University M.C. visited the crag as early as 1932 and accounted for the majority of the easier routes. The popular *Varsity Buttress* dates from this period and this route was The Stoats finest achievement. Unfortunately, further details of their activities have not been forthcoming.

In 1949, Peter Harding, while teaching at Shrewsbury Technical College, visited Pontesford Rocks with Tony Moulam, who was then a student. Their activities included ascents of established routes such as *West Wall*, *Varsity Buttress*, *Hawthorn Crack* along with repeats of several other climbs which were then known by different names; *Easy Pinnacle Route*, *Fungus Chimney* and *Fungus Slab*. At the same time they accounted for the first ascent of what is now known as *Finale Groove*.

During the 1950's and 1960's, climbers from Wolverhampton began to visit the crag on a regular basis. Most active was Walt

Unsworth who climbed many new routes, although it is possible that a number of these had been climbed previously. Stuart Thomas and Charlie Shaw also added routes of their own in this period. All of this activity was incorporated into Walt Unsworth's excellent little green guide which first appeared in 1962.

A number of short problems and eliminates have since been added. Most notably Malc Baxter led *The Superdirect* in 1962. This route still remains a bold proposition and many climbers have subsequently failed to record a true on-sight ascent. Ed Drummond has given, through his performance poetry, a very harrowing account of his ground fall whilst attempting to solo the route!

In 1986, the blank wall to the left of the upper pitch of *Varsity Buttress* was first climbed by Steve Boyden. This was also something of a "last great problem" as the route had first been top-roped by R. Tait in 1964. During the course of guidebook work for Rock Climbs in the West Midlands, Doug Kerr found and led *Trachea* in 1988.

More recently, in 1993, local climber Sion Roberts slotted in *Possum*, a worthwhile and independent pitch, just to the left of *The Superdirect.* Also of note, the flake forming Taylor's Crack on *Varsity Buttress* has now parted company with the crag to leave a slightly harder pitch.

For climbers of modest ambitions or limited experience, Pontesford Rocks have traditionally been a climbing ground of unsurpassed charm and beauty; long may this tradition continue.

THE CLIMBS

In keeping with tradition, the climbs are described from LEFT to RIGHT.

THE WEST BUTTRESS

From the col, **The West Buttress** is seen as a collection of broken slabby walls bounded by grassy terraces to the left and terminated steeply by **Grassy Gully** on the right. A narrow terrace runs across the buttress at 60ft and a fault at the left-hand end

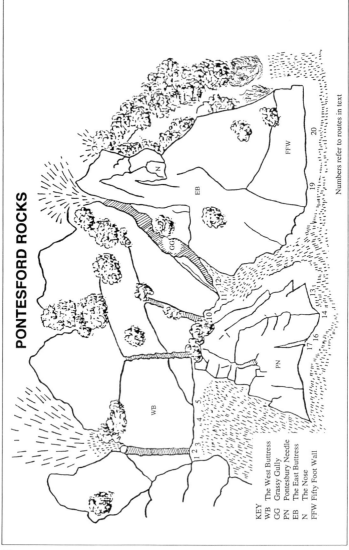

PONTESFORD ROCKS

KEY
WB The West Buttress
GG Grassy Gully
PN Pontesbury Needle
EB The East Buttress
N   The Nose
FFW Fifty Foot Wall

Numbers refer to routes in text

provides a difficult and sometimes arduous means of descent.

The first route lies just to the left of the obvious wide chimney crack of *West Crack.*

1. **West Wall**   160ft Moderate   *
    An ideal route for beginners. Popular and enjoyable.
    1.   60ft. Climb the slab keeping just to the left of the wide crack and move left after 15ft to a small ledge. Continue on large holds passing to the right of a tree to reach a large grassy ledge and belays.
    2.   100ft. Small outcrops lie above. Scramble up these passing frequent belay possibilities.

1A. **Direct Start**   4C
    Climb the thin polished slab to join the original route after 15ft.

2. **West Crack**   160ft Moderate
    This is the obvious wide chimney crack.
    1.   40ft. Follow the crack to a capstone which can be passed either on the left or climbed directly to gain a belay in the gully.
    2.   120 ft. Finish pleasantly up the broken arête on the right.

3. **Moonlight Variation**   40ft Difficult
    The edge of the right wall provides a harder alternative first pitch to *West Crack.*

4. **Eliminate G**   60ft Hard Severe 4A
    Start directly beneath the oak tree. Pull through the overlap with some difficulty and continue in a direct line on small holds to the terrace.

5. **Oak Tree Wall Direct**   120ft Very Difficult *
    A good route. Start at an obvious weakness in the overlap at the foot of a slanting rake.
    1.   60ft. Pull through the overlap at the weakness and climb for 20ft until a delicate leftwards traverse gains good holds leading up to the oak tree. Belay on the terrace.
    2.   60ft. Walk rightwards along the terrace and climb a short slab and the bulge above to gain the top.

6.   **Lower Traverse**   30ft Severe
     Start as for *Oak Tree Wall Direct* but traverse leftwards
     above the overlap to gain *West Crack*. This is a fun solo,
     slightly harder in reverse.

7.   **Right-Hand Route**   95ft Very Difficult
     Start 10ft right of *Oak Tree Wall Direct* at a small slab beneath
     the rake. Climb the slab to pull over the overlap on good
     holds. Step right before climbing directly to the upper
     ledge.

8.   **Stoats Chimney**   160ft Moderate
     This follows the broken chimney to the right. The climbing
     is relatively straightforward with numerous belay
     possibilities.

To the right, a smooth narrow slab descends to meet the path at
the col.

9.   **Last Post**   140ft Very Difficult
     This route supersedes *Magpies Nest* and *Slab Start*.
     1.   90ft. Climb the narrow slab directly up its centre,
     stepping left to climb a mossy wall to the bulge. Pull over,
     step right and then go up to a large tree and belay.
     2.   50ft. Move down and right to the arête and finish
     pleasantly up this.

10. **Wall End Climb**   175ft Very Difficult   *
     Interesting and very enjoyable climbing up the large slab
     just to the left of the gully.
     1.   70ft. Follow the right edge of the slab until a short steep
     wall is reached. Avoid this on the left and move up to belay
     on the huge oak tree.
     2.   45ft. The corner. Climb the overlapping slab behind the
     belay until a long stride to the left can be made. Move up
     and left to a tree belay on the terrace.
     2A.   30ft. Alternatively, the tricky little corner on the right
     can be climbed at Severe. This variation is known as *The
     Notch*.
     3.   60ft. Walk down and left for 20ft to reach a clean slab.

Finish up the centre of this.

11. **Finale Groove**   170ft VS   **

    The narrow subsidiary slab to the right of *Wall End Climb* provides some very good climbing.

    1.   70ft 4A. Climb the narrow slab to its end and make a tricky move left onto the main slab. Climb this to a short wall which leads directly to the large tree.

    2.   40ft. 4B. Above is a fine hanging groove. Boldly enter this from the right, or direct (harder, 4C), and follow it to a leftwards exit at the top. Tree belay.

    3.   60ft. As for the final pitch of *Wall End Climb*.

GRASSY GULLY

This is the large vegetated gully separating **The West Buttress** from **The East Buttress**. At the bottom of the gully is,

12. **Awaken**   70ft VS 5A   *

    Start just right of *Finale Groove* and follow the narrow slab rightwards to gain a short steep flake. Pull up and make a difficult leftwards 'rockover' to gain the slab above. Follow the right edge of this to finish at the large tree. High in the technical grade.

Three more routes have been recorded further up **Grassy Gully**. These are **Waltz Groove**, Very Difficult, **Subterranean**, Difficult, and **Stewball**, Severe. Unfortunately these routes are now extremely dirty and vegetated and cannot be recommended. The opposite wall of the gully is slabby in appearance but is also heavily vegetated and dirty. Several climbs have been recorded but descriptions of these routes are not included here.

PONTESBURY NEEDLE

This lies directly in front of the col. The routes are described in an anti-clockwise direction, i.e. from RIGHT to LEFT;

13. **Right-Hand Wall**   30ft Moderate

    A slight route. Start in the middle of the right-hand wall and follow the large holds rightwards.

14. **Direct Route**   60ft Severe 4A   *

Climb the rib formed at the junction of the right-hand wall and the front face until imposing bulges force a rightwards traverse to the foot of a small groove. Follow the groove to the top. A more difficult alternative finish is to climb the smooth slab to the left of the final groove at VS 4C.

15. **The Superdirect**   50ft E1 5A   *

For many years this was the 'last great problem' at Pontesford. Start as for *Direct Route* but climb directly up through the bulges above on small sloping holds. Awkward and committing climbing which, due to very poor protection, is a bold lead.

16. **Possum**   50ft E2 5B   *

A serious lead. Start just to the right of *Hawthorn Crack*. Climb directly over two overlaps and pull over the third using small finger holds. Finish leftwards through a small 'V' notch.

17. **Hawthorn Crack**   50ft Severe 4A   *

To the left there is a wide, broken groove. Follow the groove to the base of an undercut crack which is climbed with some difficulty to the top.

18. **Indirect Route**   60ft Moderate

Pick the easiest line up broken rock to gain the base of *Hawthorn Crack*. Traverse leftwards over blocks and follow large holds to the top. Alternatively, the obvious narrow crack on the right is both a better and harder finish than the original.

Pontesbury Needle has also been girdled, **Needle Girdle**, 120ft, Difficult. This provides an amusing route which starts and finishes on the summit block, the rest is left for you to discover and enjoy!

THE EAST BUTTRESS

The rambling buttress lying to the right of **Grassy Gully**. The top of the buttress is crowned by a large prominent block, The Nose, whilst the base is surrounded in trees and protected by the rather generously named Fifty Foot Wall. The approach path passes directly underneath Fifty Foot Wall and provides initial pitches for three of the routes on the buttress. The climbing here is deceptively steep and awkward; there is also some low level bouldering for the enthusiast. Believe it or not, the Fifty Foot Wall has been girdled in two pitches from left to right, **Girdle Traverse of Fifty Foot Wall**, 120ft HVS.

From LEFT to RIGHT are;

19. **Varsity Buttress**   200ft VS   *

A popular route with some interesting climbing and delightful positions on the final pitch. Start at a small clearing at the left-hand side of Fifty Foot Wall.

1.   60ft 4B. From the left-hand end of the wall, climb on good but polished holds moving first rightwards and then back left to an arête. Follow this to a belay on a small tree.

2.   70ft. A scrappy pitch. Follow the arête above to a ledge beneath The Nose. Move left to belay in a small gully.

3.   70ft. 4B. Gain the obvious scarred scoop in the left wall of The Nose, either directly or from the left, and move awkwardly right onto the arête. Finish up this in a fine position. A harder variation climbs the short steep groove just to the right, pulling over the bulge to join the original finish on the arête, VS 4C.

20. **Epiglottis**   180ft VS   *

A steep and direct line up the centre of the buttress. Start in the middle of Fifty Foot Wall beneath short twin cracks.

1.   40ft. 5A. Forceful climbing up the steep wall via the cracks gains a belay.

2.   60ft. Continue more easily up the short walls above to reach a belay on the ledge beneath the overhanging section of The Nose.

3.   80ft. 4C. *The Nose Direct*. The thin overhanging crack provides strenuous climbing onto the slab above. Follow this to a ledge and then easier climbing up the clean rib leads to the top.

21. **East Climb** 195ft Severe
Some poor initial climbing leads to a very pleasant finish in a good position. Start at the right-hand side of Fifty Foot Wall beneath a tree.
1. 35ft. Climb the broken wall via a groove to a sloping ledge. Move right along this until a slab can be climbed to a tree belay.
2. 60ft. Follow the short walls above to reach The Nose and belay on a tree which overlooks the vegetated gully.
3. 110ft. Make an exposed and delicate leftwards rising traverse across the slab to gain the rib. Finish up this.

The following two routes take direct lines on The Nose. Approach can be made via the initial pitches of *Varsity Buttress* or *Epiglottis*. Alternatively, approach by scrambling up **Grassy Gully** before traversing rightwards to the base of The Nose.

22. **Varsity Left-Hand** 25ft E2 5B *
A reachy pitch up the short blank wall to the left of *Varsity Buttress.* Unprotected and slightly harder since a small hold has broken off.

23. **Trachea** 80ft E1 5A *
Start left of The Nose Direct. The obvious overhanging arête leads steeply, with huge reaches between good jugs, onto the slab above. Follow the left edge of this to finish. The difficult initial section of this route is unprotected.

To the right of Fifty Foot Wall and at a higher level lies the rather revolting **East Gully**. To the right of this, a number of short pitches have been climbed. These include **Crow's Nest Chimney**, Difficult, **Innominate Crack**, Very Difficult, **Innominate Wall**, and **Innominate Rib**, Very Difficult. These routes are now completely overgrown and descriptions are not included. **Box Climb**, Very Difficult, lies above these routes on a small wall of clean rock, but this may prove difficult to find.

24. **Girdle Traverse**   680ft Severe

A girdle traverse has been recorded but this is now extremely overgrown in several places. It is not therefore described in full and is left for the individual to re-discover.

ISOLATED ROCKS

Level with the foot of **Pontesbury Needle,** but some distance to the left, lies a broken arête which provides **Hidden Ridge,** 60ft, Moderate. To the left of the base of *West Wall* there is a further arête with a hawthorn at its base, this is **Jackdaw Ridge,** 50ft, Very Difficult.

FAR WEST ROCKS

A group of rocks above Jackdaw Ridge which extend to the left. These are of a rather shattered nature but a few problems may be found. The summit of Earls Hill lies just above these rocks.

PONTESFORD ROCK: FIRST ASCENTS

Details of the following routes are unknown; *West Wall, West Crack, Oak Tree Wall Direct, Lower Traverse, Stoats Chimney, Right-Hand Wall, Direct Route, Hawthorn Crack, Varsity Buttress, Crows Nest Chimney, Innominate Crack, Box Climb, Girdle Traverse.*

1940's: Activity by Birmingham University Mountaineering Club. The Stoats were certainly responsible for *Varsity Buttress, Stoats Chimney* and other routes but unfortunately further details have proved to be elusive.

Finale Groove	A.J.J.Moulam and P.J.Harding in 1949, (alternate leads). Originally known as Ken's Groove.
Wall End Climb	W.Unsworth and J.Fullard, as presently described, in 1950's. The Notch Variation; traditional.
Indirect Route, Needle Girdle	W.Unsworth, who also climbed the variation finish to Indirect Route. Both 1950's.
Epiglottis	The lower two pitches are traditional. The Nose Direct was probably first climbed by C.Shaw with members of Wolverhampton M.C.
Moonlight Variation	W.Unsworth, S.Thomas and others by full moon and at about midnight, 1961
Right-Hand Route	W.Unsworth and E.Adamson in 1961
Subterranean	W.Unsworth in 1961
Stewball	S.Thomas and W.Unsworth in 1961 "Stewart made a slight mistake".
Waltz Groove	W.Unsworth and S.Thomas in 1961
East Climb	W.Unsworth and S.Thomas in 1961 Almost certainly climbed before.
Innominate Rib	W.Unsworth and E.Adamson in 1961
Hidden Ridge, Jackdaw Ridge	W.Unsworth, 1961

The publication of W. Unsworth's guidebook in 1962

The Superdirect	M.Baxter, 1962. The first lead of a 'last great problem'.
Girdle Traverse of Fifty Foot Wall	S.Wintrip and C.Shaw, 14/4/63
Eliminate G	R.Tait, 1964
Last Post	R.Tait, 1964. Other variations had previously, and subsequently, been climbed.

Innominate Wall	D.J.Haythorn. 1966. A complete mystery as this route has never received a full description or even a grade!
Sciaticus	R.Tait and D.Fryer, 23/3/67. This line contained very little new climbing and has now been incorporated into an alternative finish to Varsity Buttress.
Awaken	P.Harrison and N.Harrison, 1/3/79
Varsity Left-Hand	S.Boyden and P.Harrsion, 16/7/86. This had previously been top roped by R.Tait in 1964 and tentatively named Oesophagus; "The sheer blank wall on the left of The Nose is climbed using three small incut holds to reach for a 'jug' which will take one finger. Pull on this and mantelshelf onto the narrow ledge above."
Trachea	D.Kerr. P.Stacey and S.Grove, 5/6/88.

Publication of Rock Climbs in the West Midlands. 1988

Possum	S.Roberts (unseconded), 15/7/93. After top rope practice.

PONTESFORD ROCKS: GRADED LIST

Possum	E2 5B
Varsity Left-Hand	E2 5B
The Superdirect	E1 5A
Trachea	E1 5A
Awaken	VS 5A
Epiglottis	VS 5A 4C
Varsity Buttress	VS 4B, 4B
Finale Groove	VS 4A, 4B
Eliminate G	Hard Severe 4A
Direct Route	Severe 4A
Hawthorn Crack	Severe 4A
Last Post	Very Difficult
Oak Tree Wall Direct	Very Difficult
Right-Hand Route	Very Difficult
Wall End Climb	Very Difficult
Moonlight Variation	Difficult
West Wall	Moderate
Stoats Chimney	Moderate

IPPIKINS ROCK

OS Ref: 569965 Sheet 138 (1:50,000 Landranger Series)
With assistance from Peter Stacey.

"Two hundred yards of natural limestone outcrop, thirty to sixty feet high with a few lesser rocks. Steep, technical, treacherous in the wet and far too poorly protected. The rock is variable from the excellent to the 'treat with respect'. Well worth a visit if only to improve one's technique after a long winter, being of easy access and delightfully situated."

Charlie. Wolverhampton C.C. Journal.

SITUATION AND ACCESS

A limestone coral reef outcrop lying three miles to the south west of Much Wenlock and beautifully situated on the eastern flank of Wenlock Edge. Approach is conveniently made along the B4371 from Much Wenlock.

CHARACTER

Ippikins Rock reaches a maximum height of 60ft and offers a number of worthwhile pitches. Although some care is needed in places, the limestone is generally sound and provides some steep climbing with reliable protection. The crag is largely sheltered by trees which provide some welcome shelter during cold periods. Unfortunately, midges and wild garlic can provide intense problems on warm summer evenings. **The Main Area** and **Job Buttress** dry rapidly after rain.

ACCESS

Wenlock Edge has been designated as a Site of Special Scientific Interest due to its high geological and biological interest. Furthermore, Ippikins Rock is part of a recognised geological trail and the site is therefore of international scientific interest. Wenlock Edge, including Ippikins Rock, is owned and managed by the National Trust. Following the publication of Rock Climbs in the West Midlands in 1988 there were serious access difficulties. The National Trust became concerned at the sudden arrival of quite large groups of climbers at the crag and reacted swiftly with a ban on climbing at the crag.

In 1993 a new access agreement was reached between the National Trust, the B.M.C. and local climbers. It is **VITAL** that this agreement should be adhered to rigorously for climbing to be allowed to continue at the crag.

1. **Please climb only the routes described in the text.** A number of routes that appeared in the 1988 edition are no longer described in order to protect several rare species of plants and lichens as well as valuable geological features.

2. Please **do not** approach **Job Buttress** or the routes *Shindig* and *Digin* along the base of the crag from **The Main Area;** approach to **Job Buttress** must now be made via the field at the top of the crag.

3. **Organised groups are requested not to use the crag.** The National Trust are concerned with the use of the site by organised groups and the damage that can result to both the topsoil and the crag from repeated abseil assaults. Organised groups must therefore make use of other more suitable venues mentioned in the access section at the front of this guide.

4. Please do not park in the Wenlock Edge Inn car park; this is not a public amenity. The National Trust need regular access to the field above **The Main Area** so please do not park in the lay-by above *True Blue/Blue Groove* as this will block access via the gate. There are three suitable parking areas along the B4371;

    a) A tarmac lay-by at **The First Outcrop** and some 300 yards from **The Main Area**.

    b) Two small lay-by's some 100 and 200 yards further along the B4371 from **The First Outcrop**. **The Main Area** is accessible in a matter of minutes.

HISTORY

Climbing has taken place on a sporadic basis at Ippikins Rock over the years and local climbers have certainly used the crag as both a useful evening and winter venue. Unfortunately, further details of this activity have not been forthcoming.

In 1986, the crag was 'rediscovered' by Doug Kerr and, in the company of John Russell and Dennis Reynolds, some of the more obvious lines were re-climbed; *Dead Good* and some of the easier routes had been climbed previously. John Russell began the new route activity with his lead of the superb *Live Evil* which is certainly the best route on the crag. At the same time, Kerr was busy with leads of *Shindig* and *Digin*, employing a bolt runner for protection.

During 1987 and the early part of 1988, a number of other routes were climbed in preparation for the publication of Rock Climbs in the West Midlands. Most notable amongst there were *White Heat* and *Coming up for the Bends* by Kerr.

Following publication of the guidebook in 1988 and the resulting access difficulties, only a few further new routes were climbed at the crag. However, with a suitable access arrangement reached, the crag should now become fully established as a useful venue for local climbers.

Apart from the climbing, the area has a fascinating history; there have been numerous sightings of a ghost prowling the area and there are also tales of a rogue, Ippikin, who now apparently lies buried under the crag.

THE FIRST OUTCROP

Not surprisingly, this is the first outcrop to be reached when travelling along the B4371 from Much Wenlock. Three miles along the B4371 is a lay-by on the right-hand side of the road with a 'Beware of Cliff' sign; park here. An easy descent can be made to the base of the cliff a short distance to the right when facing away from the road.

THE CLIMBS

From LEFT to RIGHT.

Beyond a small cave is a clean, compact wall broken at the top by a grassy terrace with loose rock above.

1. **Ash Wall**   Difficult
   Start just to the left of the clean wall. Climb rightwards past a tree and scramble up the broken ledge to gain and climb a large open-book corner leading to the top.

2. **Left Edge**   VS 4B
   The wall and left arête of the clean, compact wall has a loose finish. The tree is difficult to avoid.

3. **Major's Wall**   E1 5A
   Start in the centre of the wall. Climb direct pulling leftwards around the bulge with a long reach to a miserable exit onto the terrace. Move left to finish.

4. **Major's Right-Hand**   HVS 5A
   Start in the centre of the wall and climb rightwards on good hidden holds to gain the terrace. Pleasant climbing spoilt by the leftwards exit from the terrace.

5. **Ivy Groove**   Difficult
   To the right, and before the crag disappears into ivy, follow the blocky wall into the obvious shallow groove and fight through the tree to finish.

THE MAIN AREA

This lies some 300 yards beyond **The First Outcrop**. Parking is available in two small lay-bys on the right-hand side of the road some 100 yards and 200 yards further along the B4371. Walk along the road from either of these lay-bys to reach the third lay-by. Turn sharp left at the stile and follow the muddy footpath which descends quickly to the crag.

From LEFT to RIGHT

6. **True Blue**   HVS 4C
   The projecting arête is climbed on its left-hand side before

swinging rightwards, thread runner, to finish past blue paint.

7. **Blue Groove**   Difficult
   This is the obvious slabby groove just to the right.

8. **Dan the Man**   Severe
   To the right is a black slab. This route climbs the rather vegetated, shallow rightward-trending groove at the left-hand edge of the slab. From the top of the groove finish rightwards.

9. **Black Slab**   VS 4C
   The left edge of the slab is started via a short thin crack. Continue directly past the overlap and then finish rightwards.

10. **Black Douglas**   HVS 5A
    Follow the shallow leftward-trending groove and step right to a peg runner. Pull over the overlap at its widest point and finish direct.

11. **Nothing But**   Very Difficult
    Start just to the right. Follow the wide crack awkwardly past the tree and then directly to the top. This may also be started from the left.

12. **The Whole Truth**   VS 4B
    Climb the loose lower wall to pass the large hole on the left and continue directly up to the fine finishing groove.

To the right is a distinctive, narrow pillar forming the left-hand side of an undercut wall. **Please note** that the following four routes are best served with a spare belay rope tied off to the twin trees behind the fence at the top of the cliff.

13. **The Black Hole**   E1 5B
    The centre of the pillar provides some thought-provoking and well protected climbing at the top. Climb the short, steep wall awkwardly to a small ledge at the foot of a groove. Follow the groove to finish on the left arête.

LIVE EVIL Ippikins Rock
Climber: Doug Kerr Photo: Steve Adderley

14. **White Heat**   E2 5C *
    A good, steep route up the right-hand arête of the pillar. Climb the short flake and make fingery moves past a peg runner to gain the horizontal break, peg runner. Step left and climb the centre of the pillar, peg runner, to a tricky exit. High in the grade.

15. **Dead Good**   HVS 5A   *
    The straight crack rising from the cave provides good climbing. Gain the crack directly, or from the left, and follow it past a hidden thread runner to a steep and awkward finish in the constricted groove. Low in its grade.

16. **Live Evil**   E3 5C **
    Excellent climbing on the clean wall above the cave. A problematic start over the left-hand end of the undercut gains better holds above and a peg runner on the right. Move up, thread runner on the right, and climb directly to gain good resting holds and a second peg runner. Reflect on the palindrome before finishing direct with steep fingery moves up the headwall. A direct start through the centre of the undercut provides a hard 6A problem.

17. **Coming up for the Bends**   E1 5A
    The thin crackline to the right of Live Evil. Pull carefully through the right-hand end of the undercut on large, dubious holds and follow the thin twin cracks steeply, past two thread runners, to the top. Tree belay.

18. **The Teddy Knows Traverse** HVS 5B   +
    An interesting traverse of **The Main Area** from left to right. Start as for *The Whole Truth*, and climb up and diagonally right to the small ledge on *The Black Hole*. Move delicately around the arête, peg runner, bridge across and move up to gain a standing position on a large block, on *Dead Good*. Climb rightwards across *Live Evil*, passing its peg runner, crux, to gain and finish up *Coming Up For The Bends*. Tree belay.

The next two routes can be found on a compact black wall some 80 yards to the left of **Job Buttress.** Approach to these two routes **must** be made along the top of the crag. From the information plaque at the top of **Job Buttress,** descend the wooden steps and follow the path rightwards to reach the wall.

19. **Shindig**   E3 5C

    The left edge of the compact black wall leads past a small bulge to a bolt runner. Finish with some difficulty up the blunt arête.

20. **Digin**   E2 5B

    This climbs the centre of the wall starting from behind the tree. The bolt runner on *Shindig* is used for protection.

JOB BUTTRESS

This buttress lies some 200 yards beyond **The Main Area** and almost directly in front of the Wenlock Edge Inn. Approach along the top of the crag via the field from **The Main Area**. From the information plaque descend the wooden steps and follow the path leftwards to reach the buttress.

From LEFT to RIGHT are;

21. **Dead End Job**   HVS 5B

    The undercut and overhanging arête has a difficult long reach; short and rather sharp!

22. **Little Job**   Hard Severe 4B   *

    This climbs the left-hand groove which is formed by the junction of the overhanging wall with the slabby right-hand wall. Follow the groove easily rightwards with a tricky exit onto the ledge. Sneak off leftwards to finish.

23. **Odd Job**   VS 4C *

    Start at a lower level and follow the right-hand groove with a problematic start past two thread runners. Either finish direct, rather loose, or move leftwards as for *Little Job*.

24. **In Between Jobs**   E1 5B
    A difficult start on the right-hand side of the blunt undercut arête gains a ledge on the left. Move up to gain a large hold, swing right and then finish direct.

25. **Big Job**   HVS 5A
    The centre of the wall just to the right. Pull up to stand on the ledge and climb steeply to finish up the centre of the wall above. Owing to the encroaching vegetation this is now appropriately named!

IPPIKINS ROCK: FIRST ASCENTS

Details of the following routes are unknown: *Majors Wall, Majors Right-Hand, Left Edge, Ivy Groove, The Whole Truth, Dead Good, Blue Groove, Nothing But, Odd Job, Little Job, Big Job.*

Live Evil	J.Russell, D.Kerr, 24/4/86 The leader used one rest point which was dispensed with on the second ascent by J.Russell and D.Sarkar, 25/4/86.
Direct Start:	D.Kerr (solo), 1988
Shindig	D.Kerr, D.Sarkar, J.Russell, 25/4/86
Digin	D.Kerr, D.Sarkar, J.Russell, 25/4/86
Dead End Job	D.Sarkar (solo), 1986
In Between Jobs	D.Kerr, D.Reynolds, 22/2/87
True Blue	D.Kerr, D.Reynolds, M.Sanders, 22/2/87
Black Douglas	D.Kerr, M.Sanders, 22/2/87
Dan the Man	M.Sanders, D.Reynolds, 22/2/87
White Heat	D.Kerr (unseconded), 22/4/87
Ash Wall	P.Stacey, G.Brigginshaw, 6/7/87
Coming up for the Bends	D.Kerr, R.Lanchbury, 6/12/87

Publication of Rock Climbs in the West Midlands1988.

The Black Hole	D.Kerr, P.Stacey, 31/10/92
The Teddy Knows Traverse	I.Henderson, I.Kerr, 27/3/94

IPPIKINS ROCK: GRADED LIST

Shindig	E3 5C
Live Evil	E3 5C
White Heat	E2 5C
Digin	E2 5B
The Black Hole	E1 5B
In Between Jobs	E1 5B
Majors Wall	E1 5A
Coming up for the Bends	E1 5A
Black Douglas	HVS 5A
Majors Right-Hand	HVS 5A
Dead Good	HVS 5A
True Blue	HVS 4C
Odd Job	VS 4C
Black Slab	VS 4C
Little Job	Hard Severe 4B
Dan the Man	Severe
Nothing But	Very Difficult
Ash Wall	Difficult
Ivy Groove	Difficult
Blue Groove	Difficult

GRINSHILL

OS Ref: 518238 Sheet 126 (1:50,000 Landranger Series)

SITUATION

Grinshill lies some seven miles to the north of Shrewsbury, just off the A49, and contains a rather complex series of natural sandstone outcrops and quarries.

APPROACH

From Shrewsbury, approach along the A49 and into Preston Brockhurst. Turn left at the signpost for Clive and Yorton and follow the signs into the Corbet Woods picnic area car park. Continue on foot along Upper Road, there is no access for cars, to reach **The Outcrops** and **Church Quarry.** The lower footpath from this car park leads to **The Main Quarries**.

ACCESS

The section of Grinshill known as Corbet Woods Country Park, which contains **The Main Quarries** and **The Far Quarries,** is a Site of Special Scientific Interest which is owned and managed by Shropshire County Council. The remaining climbing areas at Grinshill i.e.: **Church Quarry, The Far Rocks, Middle Rock, The Top Rocks, Lower Wall, First Upper Quarry** and **Second Upper Quarry** are on land which is owned and managed by the Hardwicke Estate.

    In recent years there has been a significant increase in the number of people using Grinshill for recreational purposes and there is now great concern with the impact of this upon the environment. In 1993 an agreement was reached with Shropshire County Council and the Hardwicke Estate for climbers to

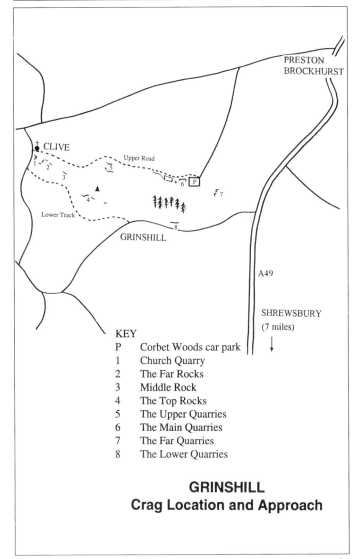

KEY

P	Corbet Woods car park
1	Church Quarry
2	The Far Rocks
3	Middle Rock
4	The Top Rocks
5	The Upper Quarries
6	The Main Quarries
7	The Far Quarries
8	The Lower Quarries

GRINSHILL
Crag Location and Approach

continue to have access to Grinshill. It is **VITAL** that this agreement should be adhered to for climbing to continue at Grinshill.

1. **ORGANISED GROUPS ARE REQUESTED NOT TO USE GRINSHILL.** Please use other, more suitable sites which are mentioned in the Access notes at the front of this guide.
2. Please do not park in Clive village. Climbers should only use the large Corbet Woods car park.
3. Climbers are requested to operate in small groups, up to a maximum of six, so as not to overcrowd the crags. Consideration should be shown for other people out walking, riding, etc.
4. Please take all of your litter home.
5. Be warned that sharp sandstone edges can easily cause serious damage to ropes and slings. When top-roping, use either a long sling or take a spare rope to protect the trees and to minimise erosion.

Whilst Shropshire County Council and the Hardwicke Estate are sympathetic to climbers it is essential that these simple access requirements are observed for climbing to be allowed to continue at Grinshill.

PLEASE DO NOTHING TO JEOPARDISE THE OPPORTUNITY OF CLIMBING IN SUCH A BEAUTIFUL PLACE.

HISTORY

The area has been used by locals for at least the past thirty years but the climbing has never been taken very seriously and records have not been kept. The text now contains a selection of traditional routes along with several new routes claimed since the last edition. There is still further potential for new routes at Grinshill and it is imagined that the area will continue to provide entertainment and amusement for local climbers and the occasional visitor.

CHARACTER

There is a mixture of quarried and natural sandstone outcrops. The quality of the rock is variable and a cautious approach is recommended; as a general rule, the darker coloured rock provides the best climbing as this is relatively compact and well weathered. The quarried exposures of lighter coloured rock are generally poor and are of little interest to the climber.

The climbing described offers plenty of variety and climbers of all grades will find routes to enjoy. The area has an intrinsic charm being a very popular local beauty spot and this helps to provide a very 'user-friendly' atmosphere. A local habitué has described the area as "like an English version of Fontainbleu" and whilst this is something of an exaggeration it does give some indication of the flavour of the Grinshill experience; accepting the limitations of sandstone climbing this is a great place for bouldering or top-roping. The crag would therefore be better described as the Shropshire equivalent of Frodsham.

The routes never exceed 55ft in length and individual pitch lengths are not included. A standard 45 or 50 metre rope will therefore be sufficient, although an additional rope is very useful (essential at **The Top Rocks**!) for arranging top ropes.

THE CLIMBS

The outcrops and quarries are described from LEFT to RIGHT (i.e. from West to East).

CHURCH QUARRY

A small, sheltered quarry lying close to Clive church, worth a visit during periods of dry weather. The quarried sandstone is reasonably sound and well weathered but the quarry floor is littered with broken glass which means that soloing and bouldering are unattractive propositions.

Approach can easily be made from Clive church by following the path through the graveyard, turning immediately right after the gate and following the footpath along the boundary wall. At a 'cross-roads' of paths continue direct and the quarry comes into view on the left after a short distance. Approach can also be made from Upper Road or alternatively by striking up the short hill from **Dangerous Cliff**.

From LEFT to RIGHT are;

1. **Mothercare**   4B
    Climb directly up the short wall beneath the large tree. A poor route.

2. **Caught in the Act**   4C
    The arête just to the right beginning on large holds and finishing with a long reach and an awkward mantelshelf onto the dirty ledge.

3. **Bill and Ted's Excellent Adventure**   5B (NL)
    The central arête is climbed on its right-hand side with precarious finishing moves to gain the ledge. Usually green and greasy.

To the right are twin converging corners forming the left-hand side of an impressive overhanging wall.

4. **Indifference of Opinion**   5B   *
    A good route. Follow the left-hand corner with difficult initial moves to gain a standing position on the small ledge. Finish more easily above.

5. **The Nebuliser**   6A   * (NL)
    The severely overhanging crack is both painful and exhausting in execution. The first few moves provide the crux; above the crack widens to accept good jams. There are unconfirmed reports that this route has been led.

6. **Whose line is it Anyway**   5C (NL)
    An interesting traverse of the overhanging wall from right to left; strenuous! Gain the rising horizontal break via the short corner on the right and follow this leftwards to join and finish up *The Nebuliser*.

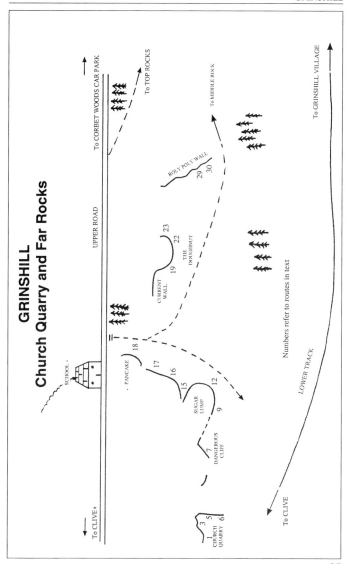

GRINSHILL
Church Quarry and Far Rocks

To CLIVE,

SCHOOL

To CORBET WOODS CAR PARK

To TOP ROCKS

UPPER ROAD

To MIDDLE ROCK

To GRINSHILL VILLAGE

ROLY POLY WALL

29

30

23

22

19

THE DOUGHNUT

CURRENT WALL

Numbers refer to routes in text

18

17

16

15

. PANCAKE

12

SUGAR LUMP

9

7

DANGEROUS CLIFF

LOWER TRACK

To CLIVE

3 5

1 6

CHURCH QUARRY

THE OUTCROPS

There are three distinctive groups of outcrops at Grinshill, these are **The Far Rocks, Middle Rock** and **The Top Rocks**. The outcrops are described from West to East. Approach along Upper road from Corbet Woods car park to reach Clive C.E. primary school. Almost opposite the school, a flight of narrow stone steps can be located which lead to the first group of outcrops;

THE FAR ROCKS

DANGEROUS CLIFF

The most westerly of the outcrops approached by following the path downhill from the stone steps, past **The Pancake**, and then rightwards and uphill beyond **The Sugar Lump**.

An approach through bracken leads to a small right-angled bay with a slabby left wall. From LEFT to RIGHT are;

7.   **Clare Has Wings**   4C
     Follow the left-hand edge of the slab as directly as the holds allow to finish over the left-hand side of the overlap on good holds. Fence belay.

8.   **Bleed With The Moon**   5A
     Start just to the left of the dirty corner. Gain the horizontal break and stand up with difficulty. Continue more easily up the slab above and finish over the overlap on good holds. Fence belay.

The dirty, thin crack in the right wall of the corner provides a 5A (NL) problem, but only the desperate need apply!

THE SUGAR LUMP

The rounded buttress passed on the approach to **Dangerous Cliff**. On the left-hand side of the buttress is a short slabby groove marked by an arrow scratched into the rock.

WHITE HEAT Ippikins Rock
Climber: Doug Kerr Photo: Steve Adderley

9. **Sugar Bullets**   5A   *
   Good climbing. Follow the short slabby groove and then step right to climb the pocketed wall. The bulge above is climbed using a pocket, trending first left and then back right to finish. Convenient tree belay.

10. **Sugar Magnolia**   5B
    Start behind the tree and follow the steep groove to gain the horizontal break below the bulge. Awkwardly gain the next horizontal break and traverse left to beneath a short, hanging flake. Pull up, gain the flake with difficulty and finish direct.

11. **Sweetie**   5A
    An interesting pitch up the blunt arête just to the right. Start immediately behind the tree and follow the arête directly. Some care is required to avoid the sharp, overhanging tree branches.

Around to the right is;

12. **One Lump?**   4C
    Gain and climb the shallow, rightward-facing groove before moving right to finish up a wide crack. More direct variations are possible.

13. **Or Two?**   5A
    This climbs the pocketed wall and bulges just to the right of *One Lump ?*

14. **Sugar Plum Hairy**   4C
    A rising traverse of **The Sugar Lump**. Climb the slabby groove of *Sugar Bullets* and traverse rightwards to a large thread runner on *Sweetie*. Step right into the groove of *One Lump* and traverse under the overlap to gain a slab. Move right and finish close to the right-hand arête.

Right again is a narrow gully which provides a convenient

means of ascent or descent. The right arête of the gully gives;

15. **Sugar Baby Love**   5C (NL)
    Climb the shallow groove in the right arête of the gully and
    finish steeply up the nose on good holds.

16. **Tate**   4C
    Start to the right of the gully and follow the short crack to
    finish directly up the dirty wall on sharp holds.

17. **Lyle**   3A
    A direct line up the slab starting some 5ft to the right of *Tate*.

18. **The Pancake**   6A
    The black conglomerate rock above the rock ledge provides
    a hard and direct problem through the widest part of the
    roof. Aspirants may find themselves as flat as a pancake on
    the rock ledge! Unfortunately, becoming rather dirty. Several
    variations exist.

To the right, past the steps and opposite to *The Pancake* is;

THE CURRENT WALL

A small and compact buttress of good rock with some interesting
bouldering on sharp holds.

THE DOUGHNUT

This rounded red buttress is the continuation of **The Current
Wall** at a lower level. The rock is generally sound and provides
a number of interesting and worthwhile routes.
On the left-hand side of the wall is,

19. **Tea Time**   5A (NL)
    Gain the short, thin crack via the wall below and finish up
    the wall above with a long reach onto the dirty ledge.

20. **Tart**   6A (NL)   *
    The green wall to the right is climbed with a difficult
    'rockover' to gain good holds in the break above. Finish
    direct with interesting moves on generally good holds.

21. **Jam**   5B   *
Start just to the right and some 20ft to the left of the right-hand arête. Climb directly up the bulging wall with an awkward finish to gain the ledge and tree belay.

22. **Cream**   6A (NL)   *
From just left of the right-hand arête climb up and then slightly left to a difficult finish on pockets.

23. **Fillo**   5B (NL)
Start right of the arête and a short distance up the gully. Pull up using sharp flakes and climb through the centre of the bulge above with a long reach to gain a good finishing hold.

ROLY POLY WALL

Lying just to the right of **The Doughnut**, this rather broken and vegetated buttress is the least attractive of **The Far Rocks** outcrops. At the left-hand side of the wall there is an obvious deep chimney.

24. **Twenty Five Ways To Eat Fish**   5A (NL)
Start just left of the chimney and climb trending leftwards up the wall to finish up a short crack.

25. **Rolling Pin**   4B
The deep chimney is a bit of a squeeze and may even leave you feeling a little bit flat!

26. **Spotted Dick**   5B (NL)
The centre of the narrow pillar just to the right of *Rolling Pin* to finish up the right arête on poor rock.

To the right there are twin grooves.

27. **Whisk**   4A
The shallow left-hand groove leads directly to the tree.

28. **Drive**   5A (NL)
The right-hand groove is followed to the roof. Use the large jammed block to finish leftwards around the roof.

The wall just to the right is crowned by an overhang but the lower wall is poor and very broken. To the right again, at a lower level, and just above the main path is a steep red/brown wall. On the left-hand side of this wall and some 5ft to the right of the tree is;

29. **Grip**   5C

Climb up to gain the right-hand side of the sloping ledge. Continue steeply up the wall to pull directly through the bulge with fingery moves and a difficult mantelshelf onto a dirty ledge.

30. **Mr Creosote**   5B (NL)

Start some 12ft to the right of *Grip* and climb up and leftwards to gain wafer-thin flakes. Move right and explode through the bulge above on surprisingly good holds.

MIDDLE ROCK

This lies some 150 yards to the right of **The Far Rocks** and approach is made by following the footpath rightwards and gently uphill from **Roly Poly Wall**. The buttress is well worth a visit as it is composed of compact and generally very good quality sandstone.

The left-hand side of the buttress is undercut by a long, low roof. From LEFT to RIGHT are;

31. **Captain Haddock**   5B (NL)

Start at the left-hand side of the roof and climb the short, leftward-trending corner. Follow the thin flaky vein above to gain good finishing holds on the right. Steep.

32. **Snowy**   5B (NL)

Pull through the bulge just to the right and trend steeply leftwards to gain the good finishing holds of *Captain Haddock*.

33. **Justin**   5B

From the top of the short, leftward-trending corner of *Captain Haddock* follow the rising horizontal break strenuously rightwards to join the finish of *Tin Tin*.

34. **Tin Tin**   5C   *

Start below the centre of the roof and make difficult fingery moves to gain the thin, fragile flakes leading steeply to big holds and a rather dirty finish.

35. **Thompson Twins**   5C

A massive reach across the roof to the right gains good finger holds on the lip. Pull up and gain the sloping ledge with difficulty. Finish more easily up the short groove.

36. **Bad**   4C

Pull though the right-hand end of the roof on good holds and follow the flakes to easier ground.

37. **Badder**   4A

A direct line up the wall just to the left of the shallow groove.

38. **Malady**   4A

The shallow leftward-trending groove is followed with some initial difficulty.

39. **Tom Tom**   4B

A direct line up the steep wall just to the right of the shallow groove on a variety of big holds.

40. **Tom Tit**   5B

Start to the left of the small tree and make difficult moves to stand on the sloping, sandy shelf. Follow the steep wall above to the overlap. Finish rightwards or more easily to the left.

41. **Caesar's Palace**   5A   **

A micro gem. From behind the small tree, climb the wall to pull over the roof on the left using huge sharp jugs. Finish direct over the smaller overlap.

42. **Brutus**   5B   *

The right-hand arête leads to the roof. Pull energetically over this to reach a large jug in the horizontal break. Finish direct over the final overlap.

43. **Midnight Madness**   5B

A poor eliminate. The steep side wall to the right of *Brutus* is climbed with a long reach from the left-hand arête to gain the finishing footholds of *Corner Climb*.

44. **Corner Climb**   4A

   Follow the left-hand corner until a finish can be made on the left wall.

A short distance to the right is a small buttress with some boulder problems.

THE TOP ROCKS

BROKEN BUTTRESS AND MAIN BUTTRESS

Lying directly in front of the triangulation and viewing points just below the summit of Grinshill, these two outcrops have a very pleasant open aspect; they receive any sunshine from early morning to late afternoon.

   A dirty gully separates **Broken Buttress** from **Main Buttress** and provides a convenient means of descent.

BROKEN BUTTRESS

Although composed of generally good quality sandstone, this buttress is rather broken and the climbing is very much of the 'go anywhere' variety. The following are a selection of the more obvious and traditional lines which provide a good concentration of lower grade climbs. The enthusiast will certainly discover further possibilities along with plenty of bouldering.

   The climbs are described from LEFT to RIGHT.

   Towards the left-hand side of the outcrop is a small clearing in the path.

45. **Evensong**   3B

   Climb directly up the wall, passing to the left of a small tree, to finish up a short nose.

46. **Morning Wall**   3A

   Start just to the right. Follow the short wall onto a large ledge and finish pleasantly via the short zig-zag crack.

The following routes begin from a rock platform up and to the right.

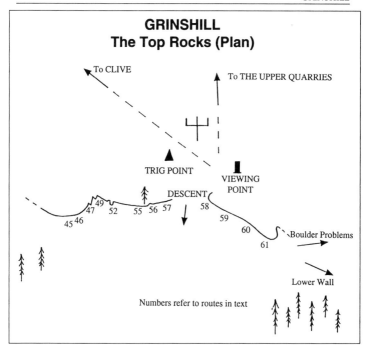

GRINSHILL
The Top Rocks (Plan)

To CLIVE

To THE UPPER QUARRIES

TRIG POINT

VIEWING POINT

DESCENT

45 46 47 49 52 55 56 57 58 59 60 61

Boulder Problems

Lower Wall

Numbers refer to routes in text

47. Dawn Corner   4B   *

The shallow groove to the right of *Morning Wall*. Gain the groove awkwardly and climb directly through the overlaps above. Good climbing.

Around to the right is a short overhanging wall with an interesting, though escapable, 5C problem.

48. Ramp   2B

The obvious slanting faultline is followed on good holds.

The sharp arête forming the right-hand side of the faultline can be climbed on its right-hand side at 4A. In the small, square-cut bay to the right is,

49. **Cockles**   5A
The thin, left-hand corner crack leads awkwardly to the square cut ledge. Finish easily.

50. **Muscles**   4A
The centre of the narrow wall just to the right.

51. **Cave Route**   4A
The steep, right-hand groove starting from a small cave.

52. **Pillar Climb**   3A
The short, square-cut pillar can be climbed from any of its three sides. Finish directly above.

To the right, at the top of the buttress, is a large tree,

53. **Ladder Crack**   3A
Climb the wide and broken crack running up to the left-hand side of the tree.

54. **Laddered Lycra**   4B
Start as for *Ladder Crack* but move right to gain and climb the short thin crack which leads to the tree.

55. **Spin on This**   5A
Climb the left arête of *Two Finger Gesture* and pull up awkwardly to gain the right-hand side of the sloping ledge. Finish up the centre of the black scoop to the tree.

56. **Two Finger Gesture**   5B
Start at the short, overhang-capped groove. Bridge up and use small pockets to gain a tiny ledge on the right. Finish direct.

57. **Pocket Route**   3A
Follow the short, pocketed wall to a ledge on the right. Step back left, as for *Two Finger Gesture*, and climb directly to the large tree.

MAIN BUTTRESS

The steep, compact buttress of good quality sandstone to the right of the descent gully which offers a number of worthwhile routes. Good belays are a long way back and a spare rope is required to arrange top-ropes.

58. **Black Arête** 5A
The short left-hand arête, just to the right of the gully, has a steep start and a rounded finish.

59. **Black Wall** 4C *
Start just to the right of the arête. Climb up to and over the bulge onto a pocketed slab. The final steepening has a good chipped hold. Pleasant climbing.

60. **Main Wall** 5A
Start behind the fallen silver birch tree. Gain and climb the shallow, leftward-trending groove and then step right. Pull through the bulge to a rounded finish.

61. **Main Overhang** 5C *
The narrow slab leads to the roof and a poor peg runner. Undercut leftwards and pull through the bulge on good holds. The final rounded mantelshelf provides the crux.

62. **Main Eliminate** 5C (NL) *
Climb the right edge of the narrow slab and move right under the overhang to finish steeply up the nose.

63. **Grinshill without Oxygen** 5A
The undercut sidewall. Start up a short, wide crack and climb steeply on generally good holds.

64. **Sidelines** 4A
Follow the bulging shallow groove lying just to the right.

LOWER WALL

Approximately 80 yards to the right, at a lower level is another wall.

65. **Wall Climb** 4B
A direct line up the pocketed wall to the left of the central, hanging groove.

66. **Central Groove** 4B
Climb directly up the wall to gain the hanging groove and follow it with moves to the left at the top.

Some 50 yards to the right of **Lower Wall** is a further buttress which gives a number of boulder problems. Approximately 200 yards to the right of this is a final buttress hidden in the trees but this is extremely dirty and broken.

THE QUARRIES

There are four groups of quarries at Grinshill but unfortunately, with the exception of **Church Quarry** which is detailed separately, these are generally poor and are of little interest to the climber. The quarries are described working from WEST to EAST;

THE UPPER QUARRIES

These are located near to the summit of Grinshill and lie approximately 250 yards to the north-east of the triangulation point. Approach is made along Upper Road from Corbet Woods car park. Follow Upper Road for just over 500 yards until a track on the left is reached; this track is blocked by a large stone and is marked by a signpost 'Motorcycling Prohibited'. Turn left and follow this track for a short distance before taking the first turn on the right to enter **First Upper Quarry**. The second turn on the right leads into **Second Upper Quarry**.

FIRST UPPER QUARRY

A vegetated and rather gloomy quarry which remains damp for long periods of time. The quarry therefore offers very little to tempt the climber. At the left-hand side of the quarry **Sands of Time** 5A (NL) climbs the obvious narrow pillar forming the left-hand side of the steep wall. Other lines exist but these await the attention of enthusiastic gardeners.

SECOND UPPER QUARRY

This quarry is also gloomy and rather vegetated. **Utter Nutter** 3C climbs the dirty, slabby corner at the left-hand side of the quarry. To the right and just beyond a large rock scar, **Shiver Me Timbers** 5B (NL) climbs the steep and impressively vegetated

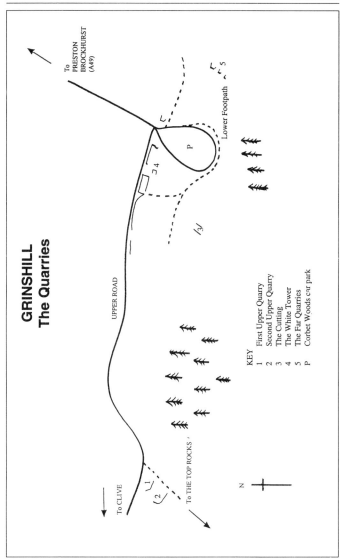

GRINSHILL
The Quarries

To PRESTON
BROCKHURST
(A49)

Lower Footpath

5

P

4

3

UPPER ROAD

To THE TOP ROCKS

To CLIVE

1

2

N

KEY

1   First Upper Quarry
2   Second Upper Quarry
3   The Cutting
4   The White Tower
5   The Far Quarries
P   Corbet Woods car park

corner beneath the large tree.

On the right-hand side of the quarry, beyond a sunken bay, are three short routes which, when dry and clean, may provide some interesting climbing. From LEFT to RIGHT these are;

67. **Nibbles**   5B

The sharp curving arête is climbed on its right-hand side. At the top great care is required to avoid the loose perched block on the left.

68. **Stitches**   5B

The blank corner directly behind the tree is climbed using the thin layback crack in the left wall.

69. **Soles**   6A

The blunt arête on the right provides fingery and technical climbing.

THE MAIN QUARRIES

These are located immediately to the west of Corbet Woods car park. There is some interesting rock scenery and an impressive deep quarried hole, **The Main Hole**, which can be viewed by peering over the wall from Upper Road. Unfortunately, the quality of the rock is generally very poor.

Approach is made by following the lower footpath from Corbet Woods car park.

THE WHITE TOWER

This isolated pillar lies roughly in the centre of the first quarried bay. Approach via the lower footpath from Corbet Woods car park and branch off rightwards from the footpath some 10 yards beyond marker post number three. **The White Tower** quickly comes into view.

70. **White Tower**   5C (NL)

The thin crack up the centre of the pillar provides good initial climbing with a difficult long stretch to pass an old peg. Gain the niche above and move left beneath an old bolt to finish more easily up the loose, crumbling twin crackline.

Tree belay.

71. **Black Looks**   5B (NL)
    The right-hand arête. Gain the small alcove and follow the
    rising, sandy break awkwardly onto the arête. Step right
    and climb more easily on the right-hand side of the arête to
    the top. Alternatively, the arête can be climbed on it's right-
    hand side throughout. Stake belay on the shoulder and tree
    belay above.

THE MAIN HOLE

This impressive, deep quarried hole lies just beyond **The White
Tower**. Follow the main footpath and branch off rightwards to
reach a viewing point at a small stone wall.

72. **Queen of the Slipstream**   6B (NL)
    The square-cut arête rising from the stone wall is climbed
    with difficulty on its left-hand side. Step off the wall and
    make a series of precarious moves to gain good holds
    beneath a small overlap at 25ft. Continue steeply on
    generally good holds. The final 15ft are rather loose and it
    is therefore advisable to lower off from below the top.

THE CUTTING

Almost opposite to **The Main Hole**, on the left-hand side of the
footpath, is a peculiar sandstone cutting which reaches a
maximum height of 25ft. The enthusiast may find some
bouldering on either of the pocketed walls but unfortunately the
rock is often green and greasy.

THE FAR QUARRIES

To the south-east of the Corbet Woods car park are three small
quarries. Follow the footpath eastwards from the car park for
180 yards until a fence is reached. This leads down and rightwards
to the base of the quarries.

The central quarry contains an obvious crack in the middle of
the back wall providing an interesting layback problem, **One**

Minute To Glory 5A, which is best top-roped owing to the unpleasant finish. These quarries provide no further routes which merit detailed description although the enthusiast may find other possibilities.

THE LOWER QUARRIES

There are also a number of quarried faces lying at the base of the woods beneath the Corbet Woods car park but these are very poor.

GRINSHILL: GRADED LIST

The routes are compared in terms of their technical difficulty.

Queen of the Slipstream	6B
The Nebuliser	6A
Cream	6A
Tart	6A
Tin Tin	5C
Thompson Twins	5C
White Tower	5C
Main Eliminate	5C
Main Overhang	5C
Whose line is it Anyway	5C
Two Finger Gesture	5B
Sugar Magnolia	5B
Black Looks	5B
Indifference of Opinion	5B
Fillo	5B
Brutus	5B
Jam	5B
Tom Tit	5B
Justin	5B
Main Wall	5A
Caesar's Palace	5A
Sweetie	5A
Sugar Bullets	5A
Tate	4C
Bad	4C
Black Wall	4C
One Lump	4C
Dawn Corner	4B
Laddered Lycra	4B
Tom Tom	4B
Wall Climb	4B
Central Groove	4B
Muscles	4A
Badder	4A
Corner Climb	4A
Malady	4A

NESSCLIFFE

OS Ref: 385192 Sheet 126 (1:50,000 Landranger Series)

"These three routes are all unique climbing experiences, the like of which I do not know of in England. All are worth three stars in national, not local, terms."

Andy Popp, 1993, referring to *Berlin Wall, Full Sun* and *Leaf Storm*.

SITUATION

A sandstone crag situated some ten miles to the north-west of Shrewsbury and lying just above the A5 at the village of Nesscliffe.

HISTORY

There is little doubt that Nesscliffe should now be regarded as a crag of national significance. However, in consideration of historical detail, it is important to recognise that the consistent trend has been for the main protagonists to keep their activities on a low profile; national publicity for the crag to the climbing world has very rarely been sought. Whether this has been a deliberate or accidental consequence remains unclear. Perhaps the persistent complications of access have contributed to this situation, but it has certainly proved difficult to establish a full historical picture.

Driving past Nesscliffe on the way to North Wales in the early 1960's, Eric Byne remarked to a casual observer that climbing had been banned by the landowner following a serious accident. This comment would seem to suggest that climbers had been visiting the crag during the 1950's. However, credit for the first recorded route goes to Pete Crew and Baz Ingle in the 1960's when they top-roped the obvious corner line in **The Main Wall Area** which later became known as *Red Square* when Ed Drummond made the first lead in 1967.

Climbers from the Midlands certainly used the crag during

the late 1960's and throughout the 1970's as a useful stopping off place to and from North Wales. At this time the remarkable corner in **The Main Quarry**, *The Pit and The Pendulum*, submitted to the tactics of the aid climber. *Cave Corner* was also climbed but unfortunately details of other climbs during this period have not been forthcoming. It is likely that routes from this period included the more obvious lines of; *Straight Talk*, *Ramblin' Days*, *Open Air* and the shorter routes to the right of **Kynaston's Cave**, such as *Pant*, *Snap* and *Short Crack.*

In the mid 1980's, activity in a modern idiom began at Nesscliffe when a small group of Shrewsbury based climbers, Nick Postlethwaite, Mike Carr and Lawrence Owen began to visit the crag on a regular basis. They began a progressive campaign of tackling the unclimbed lines and in the tradition of climbing at Nesscliffe, this activity was not taken very seriously to the extent that accurate records were not kept. At this time, the crag was owned and managed by Bradford Estates who had persistently refused to allow any climbing. It was therefore necessary for these climbers to maintain a low profile and not to attract attention to their activities. During 1985, and the early part of 1986, some of the more obvious lines were both led and top-roped, these included a free ascent of *Red Square*, *Pot Noodle* and also *Stop* (NL), *Behind the Pines* (NL) and *On the Beach* (NL) in **The Main Quarry**. In the middle of this activity, Mark Lynden paid several visits to the crag. He accounted for the first lead of an old top-rope problem to produce *Bruce Factor* and the superb *Marlene* which has become firmly established as a local classic. Both of these routes employed bolt runners for protection.

The following year saw further activity from Postlethwaite. His efforts were concentrated in the **Kynaston Cave Area** with the first probable lead of *A Sort of Homecoming* and *Road to Emmaus* (NL). The 6C barrier was broken when he eventually succeeded on the superb and highly technical *Berlin Wall* (NL). Also of note on **The Far Buttress** were *Hang Loose* and *Stay Cool*, an excellent low level traverse and *Crocodile Crack (Snapper Crack)* (NL) in **The Main Quarry**. Towards the end of this year,

Postlethwaite returned to add his final routes in the area with ascents of *The Nuance* (NL) and *Gathering Doubt* (NL). With the impending publication of *Rock Climbs in the West Midlands* these two superb routes were a fitting conclusion to this phase of development.

All was revealed in the guidebook. Many climbers subsequently came to take a look but a significant number of these were undoubtedly put off by the complications of access. A small group of very talented and capable climbers, Nick Dixon, Crispin Waddy and Andy Popp, were introduced and quickly became enamoured of the crag. Often supported by a cast of enthusiastic locals, these climbers quickly resumed development with a number of outstanding routes. Their approach to sandstone was different, after careful preparation and cleaning, routes were led in traditional style. Most of their routes relied on some in-situ protection, but never bolts. Dixons efforts in 1989 were therefore bold undertakings, for example; *Full Sun* and *Gathering Sun*. Dixon also made first leads of *Berlin Wall*, *The Nuance* and *Gathering Doubt*. At the same time Crispin Waddy climbed *Leaf Storm* and *Unnamed*, two blank corners which provided highly technical climbing. Waddy also made the first lead of *Cones and Current* which proved to be a slightly more amenable wall climb. Finally, in 1989, Johnny Dawes visited and climbed the centre of the huge wall to the right of *The Nuance*, *Ten O'clock Saturday Morning* (NL).

In 1990, Nesscliffe County Park was purchased from Bradford Estate by Shropshire County Council. Shortly after this, Shropshire County Council introduced a 'permit and pay' system for access to the crag. Despite these access requirements, further routes were climbed when John Codling made the first lead of *The Pit and The Pendulum* and contributed the bold *Notional Trust* to the wall to the right of *Red Square*. At a more amenable standard, Andy Speek climbed a worthwhile route, with a very strange name, on **The Far Buttress**.

In the summer of 1994, Dixon returned to lead the stunning left arête of *Red Square* to produce *My Piano*. Being both bold and extremely technical this outstanding route serves to indicate the further potential of the crag and with a satisfactory access agreement now negotiated between the BMC, local climbers and Shropshire County Council it will be interesting to see what the future holds for Nesscliffe.

APPROACH

Approach is conveniently made along the A5. When approaching from Shrewsbury, turn off the A5 opposite to The Old Three Pigeons Public House at a right-hand turning, signposted to Hopton. Please do not park on the wide verge immediately on the left-hand side of this lane, but use a more suitable parking area, the **Oak car park**, half a mile further up the lane. At the junction with the A5, a gate provides access to a signposted public footpath leading up to the base of the woods;

A) For **Kynaston's Cave Area** and **The Main Area** follow the footpath rightwards along the base of the woods until a left turn is taken at a signpost for **Kynaston's Cave**.

B) To reach **Main Quarry** and **Cads Leap** continue rightwards along this footpath.

C) **The Far Buttress** is best approached by turning leftwards at the base of the woods. Follow this path for approximately 250 yards before striking up the short wooded hill to reach the left-hand end of the buttress.

ACCESS

Nesscliffe Country Park is now owned and managed by Shropshire County Council. After careful negotiations, access has been secured for climbers on the following basis;

1) For access to **Kynaston's Cave Area** and **The Main Area,** approach as outlined above. **PLEASE DO NOT TAKE 'SHORTCUTS' THROUGH THE WOODS** as this will increase problems of erosion; all routes must then be approached along the base of the crag.

2) For access to the quarries, approach as outlined above.

3) **Kynaston's' Cave** is a scheduled ancient monument and English Heritage are concerned with the preservation of this unique structure. **NO CLIMBING IS THEREFORE PERMITTED FROM THE ARÊTE AT THE FOOT OF THE ROCK STEPS RIGHTWARDS TO THE END OF THE WOODEN ACCESS TOWER.**

4) Nesscliffe Country Park is extremely popular with numerous sightseers, walkers, horse riders etc. PLEASE DO NOTHING TO ENDANGER THIS ACCESS AGREEMENT or to spoil other people's enjoyment of the area.

5) Climbers should prevent damage to trees and minimise erosion to the cliff top by using long slings when top-roping.

6) Please note that there is little in the way of climbing below the 5A and 5B grades at Nesscliffe. The majority of the routes are unsuitable for organised groups who are therefore advised to use more suitable sites mentioned at the front of this guide.

CHARACTER

Nesscliffe is made up of a mixture of both quarried and natural sandstone. The rock architecture is very impressive indeed; there are huge blank walls bordered by perfect right-angled corners and square-cut arêtes. The climbing is of the steep and sustained variety, often combined with a high level of technical difficulty; there is very little to interest climbers operating below the extreme grades. Unfortunately, the quality of the sandstone, especially the more recent quarried exposures, is often variable and a cautious approach is recommended.

There is not an abundant supply of reliable natural protection and, taking this into account along with the nature of the rock, a number of routes in the text have not been led; these are denoted **NL** (**Not Led**). However, in recent years, with an increase in visitors to the crag, a number of routes have begun to receive 'regular traffic' which has helped to remove further loose material. There has also been an increasing trend for lead ascents of a number of routes; new routes that rely upon some form of fixed protection or traditional routes with sufficient

NESSCLIFFE PLAN

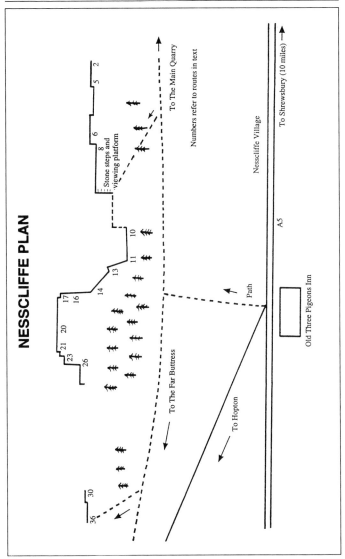

To The Main Quarry

Numbers refer to routes in text

Stone steps and viewing platform

Nesscliffe Village

To Shrewsbury (10 miles) →

A5

Old Three Pigeons Inn

Path

To The Far Buttress

To Hopton

natural protection. To incorporate this information, adjectival (ie. 'E' grades) are now included after the technical grade for on-sight ascents of all routes which have been led. This is far from being a satisfactory grading system: however it is a flexible approach that helps to reflect the problems that this crag presents. This system is not necessarily designed to encourage climbers to lead routes; leading on sandstone is a serious business, and the climber remains free to decide whether to lead, top-rope or solo. This approach helps to make the most of the crag; top-roping in itself can provide some excellent entertainment and exercise.

Recent developments have indicated that Nesscliffe can provide superb routes of the bold and 'traditional' variety. The wholesale use of 'big bolts' may well be desirable in terms of safety and enjoyment but their use, and the further development of the crag, must be given very careful consideration.

THE CLIMBS

KYNASTON'S CAVE AREA

Kynaston's Cave is a scheduled ancient monument which is easily identified by the newly constructed wooden steps and viewing platform. The climbs in this area are described working from RIGHT to LEFT, the first routes being found on the short wall 30 yards to the right of the cave containing a short, thin crack.

1. **Grounded**   15ft 5C (VS)
    A tiny problem up the wall just to the right of the thin crack. Fight through the bushes at the top or, better still, traverse off rightwards.

2. **Short Crack**   15ft 5A (VS)
    The obvious thin crack has good finger jams and holds which lead to a dirty finish into the bushes. Alternatively, escape rightwards as for *Grounded*.

3. **Snap**   25ft 5C (E1)
    Start just to the left by a shallow circular pocket. Pull up thinly and climb leftwards along the blunt flake to finish at the large tree.

4. **Pant**   25ft 5A (E1)
   From the right-hand side of the sloping ramp, climb up and
   slightly rightwards on good holds to finish up the previous
   route.

5. **Dread**   25ft 5B (NL)
   Appropriately named! The corner is climbed on its right
   wall to an exit rightwards across the bulge on appalling
   rock.

Around to the left are two grooves capped by thick undergrowth.
Harder problems, and an interesting traverse, may be found on
the pocketed wall to the left. To the left again is a recessed wall
which in turn leads to a very blank wall to the right of **Kynaston's
Cave**. Towards the left-hand side of this recessed wall is;

6. **Spitting Feathers**   60ft 4C (E2)
   Follow the short, wide crack beneath a hanging groove to
   a ledge with numerous trees. Move up and left to follow the
   slabby leftward-trending groove to its end. Step right and
   finish direct. The initial ledge may also be gained more
   directly but this remains a poor and very serious route on
   suspect rock.

7. **Drinking Gasoline**   90ft 5B (E2)   +
   The dirty groove in the right-hand arête of the blank wall
   leads to a tree. Traverse leftwards along the hanging slab
   under the overhang, above *Berlin Wall*, to a second tree.
   Climb around this and continue leftwards to the next tree.
   Finish up the short overhanging wall.

8. **Berlin Wall**   40ft 6C (E7)   ***
   The definitive Shropshire test-piece providing superb,
   highly technical climbing. Follow the short overhanging
   flake towards the right-hand side of the blank wall and
   make difficult moves to get established on the upper wall.
   Continue on tiny pockets to a desperate finish via a small
   leftwards facing flake. Two peg runners offer the only
   protection for those wishing to lead the route.

There is a short but interesting traverse from the top of the initial flake of *Berlin Wall* to a ledge low on the right at 6A. The wall some 10ft left of *Berlin Wall* contains a peg runner, two bolts and very few holds. Unfortunately there are no further details available; any takers?

The wall to the left contains a distinctive block overhang.

9. **A Sort of Homecoming**   45ft 6A (E4) *

    Gain the right-hand side of the block overhang and move left onto the horizontal break above the overhang. Make more hard moves to gain the thin crack on the right and finish directly up this past two bolt runners. Abseil off from the ledge.

As part of the access agreement climbers are requested NOT TO CLIMB ANY FURTHER ROUTES IN THE KYNASTON'S CAVE AREA. Three routes in the vicinity of the cave; *Road to Emmaus*, *Cave Corner* and *Motive Power* are no longer described and climbers are requested to avoid them.

The buttress around to the left of the cave is composed of orange coloured sandstone which is relatively poor and crumbly. No routes have been recorded here.

THE MAIN WALL AREA

Approximately 20 yards to the left is a large slabby buttress with a sandy overhang on its right-hand side.

10. **Man of Ideas**   75ft 5B (NL)

    Start on the left and move right to gain the break which runs from the left-hand side of the overhang. Finish directly up the thin and rather friable seam.

11. **Open Air**   65ft 4C (HVS)   *

    An enjoyable route following the obvious slabby left-hand arête. Awkward initial climbing leads to a pleasant finish on better holds.

Some 40ft to the left, and up a sandy bank, is a corner hidden by trees,

12. **Ramblin' Days**   70ft 5B (NL)

    Climb the corner direct past two ledges, some care being

required with a couple of insecure flakes on the right wall. Convenient tree belay.

13. **Pot Noodle**   55ft 6A (E3)

The arête to the left is closely guarded by trees and is therefore often green and greasy. A difficult start on the left-hand side gains a thin break, pull up to gain large pockets and move left to climb the thin crack. Exit over a steep and sandy bank.

The centre of the wall to the left contains a cluster of large deep pockets.

14. **Bruce Factor**   50ft 5C (E3)   **

A highly enjoyable pitch. Starting on the right climb up to gain the large pockets on the left, peg runner. Step left and climb past two bolt runners using rounded ledges. Move right to an awkward and often very dirty finish at a small, insecure, tree. It is advisable to clean the finishing holds prior to an ascent leaving the abseil rope in place to assist retreat over a sandy bank.

15. **Stay With Me**   55ft 5B (E3)   *

Start as for *Bruce Factor* but move up and rightwards as soon as possible, using good pockets, to gain and climb the shallow leftward-facing groove. Finish rightwards to avoid loose flakes and exit over a sandy bank.

Around the arête to the left is a large blank-looking wall bounded on the left by twin corners. The next route climbs this wall starting just to the right of the right-hand corner,

16. **Notional Trust**   80ft 6A (E5)   **

A bold route with absorbing and sustained climbing. Start just to the right of *Red Square* and make awkward moves to gain good holds at a large chipped letter, bolt hole. Continue direct with difficulty to reach the rising horizontal break and follow this rightwards for 20ft, to finish via a short thin crack. The route has not been led since the initial bolt and a peg runner (from the base of the thin crack) were removed; the grade assumes that both of these are in-situ.

RED SQUARE Nesscliffe
Climber: Pete Stacey Photo: Steve Adderley

17. **Red Square**   70ft 5B (E1)   ***

The right-hand corner crack provides a superb route. Not
to be missed. Good rock and excellent protection throughout.
Layback and jam the crack, past a couple of good resting
places, with the crux in the upper section where the crack
thins. A 'Thank God' tree branch facilitates a hasty exit!

18. **My Piano**   70ft 6C (E8)   ***   +

The left arête of *Red Square* provides a stunning line with
initial fierce and technical moves to pass a small overlap.
The upper section is both bold and very sustained. Four peg
runners provide only a modicum of comfort!

19. **Un-named**   70ft 6C (E6)   **

The blank right-angled corner to the left of *Red Square*
which forms the right-hand side of The Main Wall. The
crux, in the upper section, provides a very hard move and
the climbing throughout is sustained. Two peg runners
were used on the first ascent although only one of these
remains in-situ.

To the left lies the very impressive **Main Wall**. Two traverses are
of note: a higher traverse strenuously follows the line of large
pockets at 5B, the lower traverse using small finger holds is 6A.
In the centre of this wall behind the trees is;

20. **10 O'clock Saturday Morning**   6C (NL)   **

The thin seam running up the centre of the wall provides
superb, sustained and highly technical climbing. Follow
the seam with very difficult moves to gain a nest of three
large pockets. Finish directly above these taking care with
the rock on the final moves.

At the left-hand end of this wall are three corners.

21 **The Nuance**   75ft 6B (E5)   **

The right-hand corner is climbed past a peg runner until
just above half-height. Move left to gain the obvious large
handhold on the arête, and follow this, peg runner, in a
superb position to the top. A Friend 2 is useful for those
contemplating the sharp end.

22. **Gathering Sun**   70ft 6B (E7) ***

A superb and impressive route taking a direct line up the wall to the left of *The Nuance*. Boldly climb the centre of the wall to gain the thin horizontal break above the large pockets, two peg runners. Continue straight up, past a thread and peg runner in the second break, to finish up the wall above past a further peg runner in the final break. This supersedes the original route, **Gathering Doubt** 75ft 6B (E5) ** which moved right from the first break to join and finish up *The Nuance*.

22A. **Trouble in Toytown**   E5 6B ***

Superb, reachy climbing up the obvious right angled corner between 'Marlene' and 'Gathering Doubt Direct' The corner is followed in its entirety, with a brief excursion up its left arête for a few moves at two thirds height. Two pegs, friends and a couple of large nuts protect. Bold up to the first peg.

23. **Marlene**   70ft 6A (E4) ***

A very popular route and justifiably so, low in the technical grade but a bold lead. Climb the arête between the central and left-hand corners to gain the obvious cut-away. Traverse awkwardly left to climb the wall just right of the corner on pockets, peg runner, to gain a rounded ledge, peg runner. Step left and make tricky moves up the corner, peg runner, to finish.

24. **Marlene Direct**   70ft 6C (NL) **

Another excellent route which provides technical and sustained climbing. Start as for *Marlene* but continue directly up the arête. The crux involves an outlandish layback manoeuvre near the top, where some of the holds are rather sandy.

The next route can be found on the rightward facing wall to the left of *Marlene*.

25. **Cones and Current**   70ft 6B (E5) **

Gain the short thin crack in the centre of the wall and use an undercut to reach pockets in the wall above. Climb up and then leftwards, peg runner, to gain the break above. Finish awkwardly leftwards. Very good climbing.

26. **Sex and Casual Ties**   50ft 6A (E3) *
    The obvious arête to the left provides an interesting technical
    problem. A difficult start on the right-hand side gains the
    thin break on the left. Continue more easily to the top
    passing a large, dubious thread runner.

Around to the left is a slabby wall.

27. **Slapper**   45ft 5B (E1)
    Follow the short groove and swing right at the overlap. A
    long reach gains a better hold, bolt runner, and a further
    long stretch leads to easier ground.

28. **Positive**   45ft 5B (E2)
    Climb the initial groove of *Slapper* and undercut leftwards
    around the overlap. Continue with difficulty up the thin
    and dirty slab above.

29. **Dismissed**   45ft 5C (E1)
    Start to the right of a corner. Make thin moves using the
    chipped letters to gain a small ledge. Finish more easily up
    the dirty slab above. A poor route.

To the left, **Short Corner** 5C, is obvious by name and offers an
interesting technical problem. The thin crack in the left wall
provides a further 5C problem.

THE FAR BUTTRESS

This lies some 150 yards to the left of **The Main Wall Area** and
is clearly visible from the A5 lying above a sandy slope. The
quality of the sandstone is generally good, although a steep soil
bank above the right-hand and central sections of the buttress
means that several routes are rather dirty. There are however a
couple of worthwhile routes, a number of interesting boulder
problems and a superb low-level traverse.

   The climbs are described from RIGHT to LEFT. At the right-
hand end of the buttress is an undercut slab.

30. **Love Cats**   45ft 5A (E1)
    Climb up to gain the right-hand side of the slab at a small
    holly tree, step left and make delicate moves to gain a short
    flake. Avoid the loose headwall by finishing rightwards.

31. **Stuck**   45ft 5A (E1)
     Pull through the centre of the undercut to gain good but
     dirty holds above. Mantelshelf decisively and pad leftwards
     up the slab avoiding the loose direct finish.

32. **Swing The Blues**   55ft 5A (E1)   +
     A rising right to left traverse of the slab starting at its right-
     hand edge of the slab and finishing as for *Stuck*.

The slab is bounded on the left by a peculiar curving groove,
choked with a thick mound of earth. Around to the left is a long,
smooth, wall with rhododendrons at its base. **Stay Cool** 6C ** is
a superb low-level traverse of this wall following a very tenuous
line of holds; a much tried, but a seldom realised, problem.
Towards the left-hand side of this wall is,

33. **Prague**   35ft 6A (NL)
     Fingery climbing gains the right-hand side of a dirty ledge
     containing the remains of a small tree. Follow the vague
     weakness above with hard final moves to gain the dirty
     scoop.

Behind a pine tree to the left is a shallow leftward facing groove.
Starting just to the right of the groove is,

34. **In The Court Of The Sludgebaron** 35ft 5C (E3)   *
     Worthwhile but with the potential to frustrate! Boldly
     climb the right-hand side of the initial pillar and trend left
     using pockets in the wall above to gain a large hold on the
     arête, bolt runner. Use your imagination to gain the tiny
     ramp above, bolt runner, and finish up the short, dirty
     headwall.

35. **Batman**   40ft 4C (E1)
     Struggle past the tree to gain the shallow leftward facing
     groove. Follow this leftwards around the bulge taking
     great care with the rock in the upper section.

Approximately 25ft to the left and in front of the fallen tree is,

36. **Hang Loose**   35ft 6B (E3)   *
     A testing problem. Make a long stretch from the horizontal
     break to gain small pockets; a determined approach is then
     required to reach a small sandy ledge. Finish more easily
     rightwards up the dirty slab.

Some distance to the left is a final buttress hidden by trees. This is very broken and vegetated and therefore not worthy of further description.

MAIN QUARRY

This very impressive quarry reaches a maximum height of 140ft and contains a number of outstanding lines. Unfortunately, the quality of the rock is variable, the orange coloured sandstone is especially poor. The upper walls are however generally sound and provide good climbing.

Approach is made by following the main footpath rightwards from the base of the woods and the quarry quickly comes into view on the left.

The routes are described from LEFT to RIGHT.

At the left-hand side of the quarry, at the top of a short bank, is a blank corner defining the left edge of the quarry.

1. **Imagination**   25ft 6A (NL) *
    The corner provides an interesting technical problem with thin moves to gain good holds just below the top.

2. **Straight Talk**   45ft 5C (E3) *
    The obvious slanting crack in the wall to the right. Using a sloping break on the left, make hard moves to gain good jams at a small niche. The thin upper crack yields to decisive layback moves.

3. **The Pit and The Pendulum** 160ft 5C (E5) *
    The huge right-angled corner rising from the deep rubbish filled pit provides a stunning line; unfortunately, the quality of the rock for the first 40ft is very poor. There are three bolt runners and several chipped holds to assist and inspire that 'big lead' but the climbing is sustained throughout.

4. **Full Sun**   150ft 6B (E6) ***
    The magnificent arête to the right of *The Pit and The Pendulum*. To quote the second ascentionist; "one of the most striking single pitch lines in England". From the sloping bank climb the difficult thin crack on the right of the arête to a good resting ledge. Continue on the right, using the arête and a thin seam, to pull around to the left to a slab and a further rest.

Follow the bold, left curving flake on the headwall before pulling back right to finish up a thin twisting crack just left of the arête. Superb and sustained climbing which remains fairly bold despite numerous peg runners.

5. **Leaf Storm** 140ft 6B (E6) ***
The perfect, right-angled corner just to the right of *The Gathering Sun* provides a 'Super Nectar'. Climb the initial difficult corner to some good horizontal breaks. A bewildering 15ft crux section of pure stemming ensues until it is possible to pull out of the groove and climb up the old chipped letters on the right wall. Finish via the easier upper groove. The route was protected by several peg runners which are now missing.

The wall to the right is approximately 100ft wide and bounded to the left by a large fallen slab. The quality of the rock here is generally very good but unfortunately the following three routes have suffered from a lack of attention in recent years and are now becoming rather green and vegetated. The first route can be found roughly in the centre of the wall and behind the large, overbearing pine tree.

6. **Behind the Pines** 120ft 6B (NL) *
Use square cut holds to gain the thin flake leading to a niche. Move up and right and make a hard move to gain the horizontal break. Fine climbing up the left side of shallow grooves leads to a finish up the slabby wall.

7. **On The Beach** 110ft 6A (NL) *
Start behind a smaller tree 30ft to the right. Climb the crack to a small ledge and make hard moves up to the bulge. Either climb directly on pockets or move left and climb the short groove before finishing up the slabby headwall.

8. **Stop** 110ft 6A (NL)
Start 20ft to the right of *On The Beach* and climb the short mossy slab to a vegetated ledge. Move up to a leftwards sloping niche and follow the flake crack to its end. Hard moves on pockets lead to an overhung ledge. Gain the blunt

flake above and trend rightwards to finish or, alternatively, move left using sloping holds, harder.

Around to the right is a blank corner. The thin crack system to the right of this is;

9. **Crocodile Crack (Snapper Crack)**   70ft 6B (NL)
Follow the thin cracks to gain the horizontal break via hard moves on crumbling holds. Move left and follow the flake crack to its end. A hard move, or dyno, gains a good hold at the base of the final crack which leads, carefully, to the top.

10. **Happy Talk**   30ft 5A (NL) +
The blunt, S-shaped arête in the wall on the right. Climb the arête starting on the right to a sloping ledge. Move left using pockets and finish carefully up the thin crack.

The arête up and to the right provides a short problem.

CADS LEAP

Reaching a maximum height of 70ft this secluded quarry is a rather unattractive place. There are numerous trees on the quarry floor which shade the quarry and leave it damp for long periods.

   Approach by following the footpath until approximately 50 yards beyond **The Main Quarry** and then take the path which forks off to the left. The quarry is entered via a small rock cutting. From LEFT to RIGHT are;

1. **Barabadabada**   70ft 5C (NL) +
This is the left-hand corner facing the rock cutting. Start some 5ft left of the corner and climb bearing rightwards to the shelf. Finish up the shallow corner and crack.

2. **Jungle Tips**   40ft 5A (NL) +
Climb the steep right-hand corner and flake crack, the base of which is gained by scrambling up the easy angled rock ledge.

SMACK THE JUGGLER Llanymynech Quarry
Climber: Gary Gibson Photo: Hazel Gibson

NESSCLIFFE: FIRST ASCENTS

Details of the following routes are unknown; *Ramblin' Days, Straight Talk, Open Air, Sex and Casual Ties, Grounded, Short Crack, Pant* and *Spitting Feathers.*

Red Square	P.Crew and B.Ingle, (NL) 1960
	First lead, E.Drummond and R.Llewellyn, July 1967. One point of aid,
	"a sling was used in the upper, thinnest part of the crack".
	First free ascent N.Postlethwaite 1986, but possibly done before.
Cave Corner	E.Edkins and B.Davies, 23/7/66. Three points of aid.
	First free ascent unknown. Not described in text.
The Pit and the Pendulum	E.Edkins and H.J.Richards, 1/8/66. At HVS/A2 this was predominantly an aid route involving the use of both pegs and wooden wedges;
	"twelve feet from the top the crack widens and is free climbed, strenuously".
	The chipped holds are traditional. A number of bolt runners appeared on the lower section in the early 1980's. First free ascent N.Dixon, (NL) 1988.
	First lead J.Codling, June 1990,
	"Replaced 2 of 3 bolts. Very loose to start with, upper ³/₄'s brilliant and E1".

More activity by local climbers during the late 1960's and 1970's. Routes from this period almost certainly included; *Straight Talk, Ramblin' Days, Open Air* and some of the shorter routes to the right of **Kynaston's Cave**.

Barabadabada	N.Postlethwaite and L.Owen, 1985
Jungle Tips	N.Postlethwaite and L.Owen, 1985
	Both of these routes may have been climbed previously.
Motive Power	N.Postlethwaite, (NL) 1985. Not described in text.
Man of Ideas	M.Carr, (NL) 1986
Pot Noodle	N.Postlethwaite, 1986
Behind the Pines	N.Postlethwaite, (NL) 1986

On the Beach	N.Postlethwaite, (NL) 1986
Stop	N.Postlethwaite, (NL) 1986
Bruce Factor	M.Lynden and N.Craine, 12/4/86
	The first lead of an old top-rope problem.
Drinking Gasoline	M.Lynden and S.Smith, 28/4/86
Marlene	M.Lynden and B.Craig, 28/4/86
	A superb discovery which has seen many local ascents.
	First led without clipping the bolt runner in 1989, this has now been removed.
Slapper	J.Cort and S.Silcock, winter 1986
	Two bolt runners were placed but the lower one has been removed.
A Sort of Homecoming	N.Postlethwaite, 1987
	Probable first lead. The two bolt runners subsequently appeared in 1989.
Road to Emmaus	N.Postlethwaite, (NL) 1987
	This was led as far as the window of Kynaston's Cave, the peg runner was already in place. The loose upper groove required a top-rope. Not described in the text.
Hang Loose	N.Postlethwaite, 1987
Stay Cool	N.Postlethwaite, 1987. The completion of a superb and highly technical low level traverse of **The Far Buttress**.
Berlin Wall	N.Postlethwaite, (NL) 1987
	"About as easy as its namesake!"
	The chipped hold is traditional.
	First lead N. Dixon summer 1989. Two peg runners were placed.
Crocodile Crack	N.Postlethwaite, (NL) 1987
Happy Talk	N.Postlethwaite, (NL) 1987
Dread	D.Kerr, (NL) 15/8/87
	Only the desperate need apply!
Positive	D.Kerr, (solo) 15/8/87
Dismissed	D.Kerr, (solo) 15/8/87. A poor route not included in the 1988 guide.
Stuck	D.Kerr, (solo) 27/9/87
Batman	A.Brown, (NL) 27/9/87
The Nuance	N.Postlethwaite, (NL) 1987
	First lead N.Dixon, summer 1989. One new peg runner was placed.

Gathering Doubt	N.Postlethwaite, (NL) 1987
	First lead N.Dixon, summer 1989, since
	superseded by *Gathering Sun*.
Love Cats	J.Cort, 20/4/88
Swing the Blues	J.Cort, 20/4/88
Stay with Me	J.Cort, 21/4/88
	Previously known as *Sheila Factor*, a much
	more appropriate name!
Prague	N.Dixon, (NL) 1988

Publication of Rock Climbs in the West Midlands, 1988.

Full Sun	N.Dixon, B.Anderson, A.Brown, S.Harland
	and G.Taylor, Spring 1989. A stunning line
	and a magnificent discovery.
Leaf Storm	C.Waddy, Spring 1989
Gathering Sun	N.Dixon, B.Anderson, A.Brown, 25/4/89
Un-named	C.Waddy, Summer 1989

These routes, and the leads of *Berlin Wall*, *The Nuance* and *Gathering Doubt*, represented a significant advance in local standards. At the same time, Andy Popp was active with second ascents of *Full Sun*, *Leaf Storm* and *Berlin Wall*.

Cones and Current	Unknown (NL).
	First lead C.Waddy and J.Biddle, Summer 1989
Marlene Direct	N.Dixon, (NL) Summer 1989
Ten O'Clock Saturday	
Morning	J.Dawes, (NL) 1989
	"Nesscliffe, that undeveloped 'just waiting for
	new routes' crag".
Notional Trust	J.Codling, 14/7/90
In the Court of the	
Sludgebaron	A.Speek, 13/10/90
My Piano	N.Dixon, June 1994. After top-rope practice.
	A major line and a grand addtition!
Imagination	S.Adderley, (NL) 1/7/94
Trouble in Toytown	J.K.Porter, 18/4/95

NESSCLIFFE: GRADED LISTS

Technical difficulty:		Overall difficulty:	
My Piano	6C	My Piano	E8 6C
10 O'Clock Saturday Morning	6C (NL)	Berlin Wall	E7 6C
Stay Cool	6C	Gathering Sun	E7 6B
Berlin Wall	6C	Full Sun	E6 6B
Marlene Direct	6C (NL)	Un-named	E6 6C
Un-named	6C	Leaf Storm	E6 6B
Gathering Sun	6B	The Nuance	E5 6B
Leaf Storm	6B	Notional Trust	E5 6A
Full Sun	6B	Gathering Doubt	E5 6B
The Nuance	6B	Trouble in Toytown	E5 6B
Trouble in Toytown	6B	Cones and Current	E5 6B
Behind the Pines	6B (NL)	The Pit and The Pendulum	E5 5C
Hang Loose	6B	A Sort of Homecoming	E4 6A
A Sort of Homecoming	6A	Marlene	E4 6A
On The Beach	6A (NL)	Pot Noodle	E3 6A
Prague	6A (NL)	Hang Loose	E3 6B
Stop	6A	Sex and Casual Ties	E3 6A
Pot Noodle	6A	In the Court etc	E3 5C
Sex and Casual Ties	6A	Straight Talk	E3 5C
Marlene	5C	Stay With Me	E3 5B
Bruce Factor	5C	Bruce Factor	E3 5C
In the Court of the Sludgebaron	5C	Positive	E2 5B
Straight Talk	5C	Red Square	E1 5B
Snap	5C	Snap	E1 5C
Stay With Me	5B	Slapper	E1 5B
Red Square •	5B	Pant	E1 5A
Positive	5B	Stuck	E1 5A
Slapper	5B	Open Air	HVS 4C
Pant	5A		
Short Crack	5A		
Stuck	5A		
Open Air	4C		

HARMERHILL

OS Ref: 475277 Sheet 126 (1:50,000 Landranger Series)

SITUATION AND APPROACHES

Some eight miles to the north of Shrewsbury there are two
sandstone quarries at Harmerhill. Approach via the A528 from
Shrewsbury. Turn left at the Bridgewater Arms public house
and then left again just after the Red Castle public house onto
Lower Road.

ACCESS

The question of access is uncertain, although there have been no
difficulties to date. PLEASE NOTE THAT INCLUSION OF THE
FOLLOWING ROUTES IN NO WAY IMPLIES THAT
CLIMBERS HAVE A RIGHT TO CLIMB HERE.

CHARACTER AND HISTORY

The quarried sandstone at Harmerhill is variable in quality and
care must be exercised as there has already been one serious
accident owing to loose rock. Development at Harmerhill began
in 1985 when local climbers from Shrewsbury added the
following routes.

THE FIRST QUARRY

This rather dismal quarry lies hidden in the trees and can be
difficult to locate. It should not be confused with the other
quarry, on private land, which is passed on the approach along
Lower Road. Follow Lower Road for just under one mile until a
white house is reached on the left-hand side of the road. This
white house is opposite to a private driveway and a signposted
public footpath on the right-hand side of the road. Parking here

is very difficult and it would be sensible to proceed along Lower Road until a more convenient spot is located. Follow the public footpath which skirts leftwards behind the private driveway and break off rightwards after approximately 100 yards to enter the quarry.

THE CLIMBS
From LEFT to RIGHT.
The left-hand side the quarry forms a circular recess. In the right wall of this recess is a distinctive narrow pillar.

1. **Pugwash Mouthwash**   30ft 5A (NL) +
   The twisting crack running up the left-hand side of the pillar.

2. **Harmless**   30ft 5A (NL)
   In the smooth wall around to the right, gain and climb the obvious crack which widens towards the top.

3. **Harmfull**   30ft 5B (NL)
   The faint green arête/rib some 20ft to the right.

To the right, past a green slab and at a lower level, is a long, smooth wall. This wall is broken by a jumble of grooves at the right-hand end. To the right again and up the bank is;

4. **The Anchor**   40ft 5B
   The wide, crumbly crack with a dog-leg is steep.
   Set at a slightly lower level is a square-cut recess containing a gently overhanging wall.

5. **Sling Your Hook**   45ft 5B
   Follow the left-hand corner and break out leftwards up the steep side wall via the thin crackline. It is also possible to finish directly up the corner.

THE ROAD SIDE QUARRY
This lies some 300 yards beyond **The First Quarry** and is obvious by name. Continue along Lower Road to reach a small, grassy lay-by on the right-hand side of the road. This lay-by is opposite a left-hand turning for Webscott Farm. The quarry is

entered via the steps leading up from the lay-by.

THE CLIMBS

From LEFT to RIGHT.

6. **Corner Climb**   25ft 4C
   Climbs the slabby left-hand corner of the twin corners on poor rock.

7. **Tim's Tumble**   50ft 5C (NL)
   The impressive left-hand corner of the sunken bay. Steep climbing leads past a bulge and hanging flake to a strenuous finish. Some care required with the rock.

To the right **Why Bother?** 20ft 5A (NL) climbs the short flake crack from the ledge in the centre of the upper wall. Gain the ledge via abseil and then ponder the logic of the route name!

8. **Jubilee Principle**   40ft 6B (NL) **
   The square-cut arête springing from the sloping bank is climbed on its right-hand side. Gain the arête from the right and continue via hard laybacking until useful layaways on the right allow a small ledge to be gained. Finish easily. An excellent, technical route, which is well worth searching out.

The final route is provided by **Cheese Crack** 30ft 5A which follows the dirty and widening crack at the right-hand end of the wall just to the left of the blank corner.

STIPERSTONES

OS Ref: 367986 Sheet 137 (1:50,000 Landranger Series)

SITUATION AND CHARACTER

> "Above the Stiperstones Inn the moor rises in great swellings of turf, deeply cut by the little side valleys. On the crest however, there is an unusual line of rock pinnacles extending for several hundred yards...."   *W. Unsworth 1962.*

This then is the Stiperstones. The scenery here is more in keeping with the Dartmoor Tors than with the Shropshire hills. In gathering darkness or in misty conditions it can be a spooky place. Legend has it that a sighting of Eric the Red, the headless horseman, means that the country is on the verge of war!

The pinnacles and outcrops provide several short but worthwhile routes and there is plenty of bouldering. The quartzite rock is well weathered and generally sound. A visit to Stiperstones is easily combined with a trip to Pontesford Rocks.

APPROACH

The normal approach is made from the A488, the Shrewsbury to Bishop's Castle Road, via Snailbeach and then the village of Stiperstones. There is a car park at the southern end of Stiperstones, close to Cranberry Rock.

THE CLIMBS

These are described working from SOUTH to NORTH.

CRANBERRY ROCK

This is the first outcrop to be reached when approaching from the car park, although the outcrop faces west so is not immediately visible. There are two slabby grooves and these may be of some interest to the beginner. From RIGHT to LEFT are;

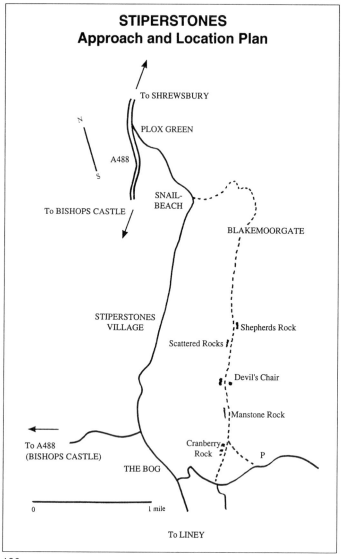

STIPERSTONES
Approach and Location Plan

To SHREWSBURY

N

S

PLOX GREEN

A488

SNAIL-BEACH

To BISHOPS CASTLE

BLAKEMOORGATE

STIPERSTONES
VILLAGE

Shepherds Rock

Scattered Rocks

Devil's Chair

Manstone Rock

To A488
(BISHOPS CASTLE)

Cranberry
Rock

P

THE BOG

0   1 mile

To LINEY

1. **Fossil Arête**   Moderate
   The broken arête to the right of the right-hand groove.
2. **Central Route**   Moderate
   Climb the right-hand groove.
3. **Original Route**   Moderate
   The left-hand groove.
4. **Cranberry Wall**   Moderate
   Climb the rather broken wall around to the left.

Some 15 yards to the left lies a pleasant slab,

5. **Glass Slab**   Difficult
   The clean and narrow slab on the right is quite polished.
6. **Steps**   Moderate
   The obvious left to right diagonal line.
7. **Ordinary Route**   Moderate
   Gain and climb the shallow hanging groove.

MANSTONE ROCK

The broken buttress underneath the triangulation point, the second highest point in Shropshire. A few small problems may be found.

THE DEVIL'S CHAIR AREA

Approximately 150 yards to the South of **The Devil's Chair** is a small buttress with several interesting short problems. From RIGHT to LEFT are;

8. **Right Wall**   5B
   This climbs the brown wall on the right with a long reach to finish.
9. **Central Wall**   4A
   A good climb following the central line of weakness.
10. **Eric's Arête**   5A
    The undercut arête is split by a sloping ledge and has a difficult start.
11. **Eric's Crack**   4C
    Climb the thin but widening crack around to the left.

12. **Central Crack**   4A
    The thin crack left again.

13. **Short Arête**   4B
    Follow the short left-hand arête, suprise, suprise.

14. **Corner Climb**   Difficult
    Climb the shallow corner groove in the right-hand gully
    wall.

15. **Glaze**   Very Difficult
    The slab across the gully is climbed using large sloping
    holds.

Some shorter problems may be found to the left.

THE DEVILS CHAIR

This lies just to the north and reaches a maximum height of 45ft.
Although rather broken in nature there are several worthwhile
pitches. From LEFT to RIGHT are;

16. **Devils Corner**   Very Difficult
    A good route following the obvious rightward-facing corner
    crack set above a narrow slab.

17. **Right Corner**   Difficult
    The mirror image of *Devils Corner* is both shorter and wider.

To the right is a broad tower bounded on its right-hand side by
a broken chimney.

18. **I'd Rather Be The Devil**   VS 4C
    The steep left-hand arête is quite exciting.

19. **Devils Tower**   VS 4A
    Climb the short slab and pull leftwards around the bulge.
    Finish rightwards up the blocky tower.

20. **Sit Down!**   VS 5A
    The slender slab leads pleasantly to the overlap. A very
    long reach gains good finishing holds in the blocky groove.
    Stepping right beneath the overlap reduces the grade.

21. **Devils Chimney**   Moderate
    A route of some historic interest following the broken
    chimney beneath the archway. Unfortunately there is little
    else of interest!

OTHER CRAGS

Middletown Quarry
OS Ref: 288119 Sheet 126 (1:50,000 Landranger Series)
A dolerite quarry lying on private land just above the village of Middletown on the A458. After passing through Middletown, travelling from Shrewsbury, a small lane on the right leads up to two houses. Park by the gate on the left and follow the track into the quarry. The quarry is some 180ft in height but the rock is very friable. There is a large slab and steep wall in the right-hand corner of the quarry. **Degeneration Game** 165ft, E1 5A, takes a direct line up the slab above the scree fan. Descent from this route is made by abseil from bolts.

Polesgate Quarry
OS Ref: 391047 Sheet 126 (1:50,000 Landranger Series)
A small secluded quarry which offers some potential for the enthusiastic expert. Approach via the A488 from Shrewsbury. Turn left opposite to the church in Pontesbury and follow the sign marked Pontesbury hill. This lane leads to a small parking area after one mile. Take the right-hand path past a single wooden bar gate to reach the quarry after approximately 400 yards. There is an interesting looking slab towards the back of the quarry which could yield two or three worthwhile routes after some careful preparation. The slab has apparently been top-roped by local climbers. The question of access is unknown.

More Quarry
OS Ref: 325935 Sheet 137 (1:50,000 Landranger Series)
Another quarry lying on private land just above the A488 some four miles to the north of Bishop's Castle. Approach from the road via the steps leading up from the concrete retaining wall. To reach the upper quarry follow the footpath which leads up and around to the right of the lower quarry. The slab on the left-hand side of the upper quarry is taken by **Can't Stop** E2 5C. To

the right there is a steep green slab. **Green Crack** VS 4C + climbs the crack and overhang on the left hand side of the slab. **Slab and Corner** VS + follows the centre of the slab before moving right into the corner and finishing up the arête. **Another Tick in the Book** HS 4B follows thin cracks in the slab around to the right to finish up a short corner.

Fairy Glen Quarry (Wrekin Quarry)
OS Ref: 638092 Sheet 127 (1:50,000 Landranger Series)
Lying at the base of The Wrekin, Fairy Glen Quarry is a popular and suitable location for organised groups. Leave the M54 at junction 7 and head south on the minor road sign-posted for "Little Wenlock and The Wrekin". After one mile there is parking at a T-junction and the quarry is seen on the left-hand side of the road.

High Rock
OS Ref: 725940 Sheet 138.(1:50,000 Landranger Series)
High Rock is a large crumbling sandstone crag lying half a mile to the north of Bridgnorth just above the A442. High Rock reaches a maximum height of 110ft and is used by Scouts and other groups for abseil practice. Several climbs have been recorded here but owing to the unreliable nature of the rock they are not described.

Worcestershire

SOUTHSTONE ROCK (THE HERMITAGE)

OS Ref: 709640 Sheet 138 (1:50,000 Landranger Series)

LOCATION AND APPROACHES

This Coralian limestone outcrop lies three miles to the south-west of Great Witley. Approach can be made from Stourport-on-Severn via the A451 from Kidderminster. Continue west along the B4203 from Great Witley as far as Stanford Bridge. Turn left once over the river towards Shelsey Walsh. Follow this road for one mile to reach a small layby on the left-hand side of the road, this layby is opposite to the remnants of a rusty, corrugated iron barn; limited parking. Pass through the gate on the right and follow an indistinct public footpath, next to a tiny stream, over a second gate and into the woods. Continue up the footpath, taking the left-hand fork in the path, and struggle past a fallen tree to reach the crag.

ACCESS

Although the question of access is unknown, there have been no difficulties to date. Please note; THE INCLUSION OF THIS CRAG, OR THE ROUTES UPON IT, IN THIS GUIDEBOOK DOES NOT MEAN THAT ANY MEMBER OF THE PUBLIC HAS THE RIGHT OF ACCESS TO THE CRAG OR THE RIGHT TO CLIMB UPON IT.

CHARACTER

It is difficult to adequately describe the character of this crag, save to say that the atmosphere and ambience here are unique. For many, including the author, it is a rather frightening and inhospitable place - rumours that the site is used for witchcraft are entirely plausible!

The bulk of the climbing is concentrated on **The Main Face**, a large pinnacle reaching a maximum height of 50ft, which provides several steep routes on generally very good holds. Whilst the rock is surprisingly good and relatively solid, the rather brittle nature of the limestone does not inspire full confidence or trust, especially for the placement of runners. Unfortunately, the three main routes have a very dirty and unstable finish and it is therefore necessary to pre-place a belay rope to overcome this. The problem is also experienced on other routes and it has certainly hindered the further development of the crag, **Back Canyon** has several interesting looking lines but the unpleasant nature of the finishes is very off-putting. For these reasons, many climbers simply prefer to top-rope and there is certainly some entertaining and strenuous climbing at hand.

HISTORY

Southstone Rock, known locally as The Hermitage, was discovered by members of Worcester M.C. in the early 1980's. Unfortunately, it is unclear whether any routes where recorded at the crag by members of this club as no further details have been forthcoming. Acting on a tip-off, Doug Kerr eventually stumbled onto the crag in the summer of 1986. With the help of John Russell, probable first leads of the routes on **The Main Face** were made. In the same year, Peter Stacey climbed a couple of further routes and development was brought to a close with the publication of Rock Climbs in the West Midlands in 1988.

Over recent years, Southstone Rock has seen a steady increase in visiting climbers and several new routes have been added. Of some note, Toby Archer discovered *Flight Of The Fruit Bat*, an unusual and worthwhile pitch, in September 1991. The full potential has yet to be realised and accepting the limitations of the crag a number of challenging lines remain for enthusiastic locals.

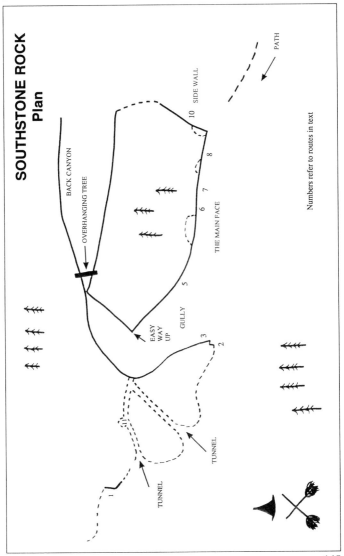

SOUTHSTONE ROCK
Plan

BACK CANYON

OVERHANGING TREE

EASY WAY UP

GULLY

THE MAIN FACE

SIDE WALL

10

8

7

6

5

3

2

1

TUNNEL

TUNNEL

TUNNEL

PATH

Numbers refer to routes in text

THE CLIMBS

These are described from LEFT to RIGHT and in an anti-clockwise direction.

Approximatley 30 yards to the left of **The Main Face,** set at a slightly higher level, is a short, leftwards-facing wall,

1. **Winters End Wall**   VS 5A +
    Climb the right arête before moving leftwards to finish up the centre of the wall. Due to the loose and unpleasant finish it is advisable to lower off from the small trees just below the top.

THE MAIN FACE

2. **Freudian Arête**   Hard Severe 4C   +
    The undercut arête to the left of *Aside*. Pull over the undercut and follow the loose and vegetated arête above

The rib just to the right provides *Reefer* VS 5A + which moves right to join and finish as for *Aside*.

3. **Aside**   VS 5A
    This is the short overhanging wall facing *Scoop Wall*. Good holds lead steeply to a twin sapling at the top and a scruffy finish.

4. **Short Sharp Rock Treatment**   VS 5A +
    Start as for *Aside* but trend diagonally rightwards to below a large block. Continue rightwards below this to finish.

5   **Scoop Wall**   VS 4B
    Start to the right of the gully. Follow the short wall into the circular scoop. Pull through the bulge above to gain the headwall which leads to a tree belay.

To the right is a huge undercut nose sporting a mysterious thread runner. Just to the right is a deep chimney.

6. **Madonnas Groove**   HVS 5A
    Climb easily up the chimney to a ledge on the left. Bridge outwards and rightwards before stepping down to cross the overhanging wall to gain the short finishing ramp. A pre-placed belay rope is required to overcome the unpleasant finish.

146

Just to the right is a small, undercut nose.

7. **Physical Attraction**   E2 5C
   Pull over the undercut and stand up with difficulty in the
   letter box. Move up to a port-hole pocket, thread runner,
   and cross the overhanging wall rightwards to finish as for
   the previous route. A pre-placed belay rope is required.

8. **Over and Over**   E1 5B
   Climb through the right-hand side of the cave and follow
   the leftward trending line to a small resting ledge. Continue
   steeply on undercuts to finish. A pre-placed belay rope is
   required.

9. **Move On Up**   HVS 5A
   Start 10ft right of *Over and Over* and climb the deep chimney
   to a good nut placement. Pull out right and follow the
   chimney rightwards onto the side wall. Finish up this.

SIDE WALL

The wall around to the right: unfortunately the rock is rather
dubious and dirty.

10. **Whinger**   VS 4B
    The right-hand edge of the wall above the undercut leads
    to a dirty finish and a tree belay. An alternative start can be
    made from the left-hand side of the undercut.

BACK CANYON

The deep, dark gully behind **The Main Face**. The left-hand wall
offers several steep possibilities and a strenuous low-level
traverse at 5A. On the slabby, right-hand wall, three routes have
been recorded in the area of the flowstone beneath the
overhanging tree. Due to their dirty and vegetated nature they
cannot be recommended.

   Now for something completely different. The final route is
approached from **The Main Face.** From beneath *Scoop Wall,*
follow the gully to its end and enter the right-hand tunnel.

11. **Flight Of The Fruit Bat**   Difficult
Interesting and atmospheric. From the end of the tunnel,
clamber up the chimney until it is possible to finish through
the obvious skylight.

SOUTHSTONE ROCK FIRST ASCENTS

Scoop Wall	J.Russell, D.Kerr, 8/7/86
Madonnas Groove	J.Russell, D.Kerr, 8/7/86
Over and Over	J.Russell, D.Kerr, 8/7/86
Physical Attraction	D.Kerr, J.Russell, 8/7/86
	Probable first ascents of four obvious lines. All of the routes were equiped with in-situ thread runners but these were removed shortly afterwards by unknown climbers.
Whinger	P.Stacey, A.Mills, 1986
	Alternative start; R.Abraham, T.Archer, M.Hardine April 1991.
Move on Up	P.Stacey (unseconded), 24/4/87
Aside	Traditional.
Reefer	A.Roberts, I.Roberts, 15/4/89
Flight Of The Fruit Bat	T.Archer (solo), September 1991
Short Sharp Rock Treatment	T.Archer (solo), 26/3/93
Winters End Wall	T.Archer (solo), 29/3/94
Freudian Arête	T.Archer (solo), 29/3/94

THE MALVERN HILLS

By Roger Smith and Doug Kerr

INTRODUCTION

The long whaleback ridge of the Malvern Hills is a very popular attraction for walkers and ramblers, indeed, the walk of the length of the hills from Chase End to North Hill is one of the finest in the south of England. There are several quarries and small outcrops scattered along the length of the hills, but unfortunately these offer very little to tempt the serious rock climber. **Ivy Scar Rock** has some local popularity with both beginners and organised groups and provides the best concentration of climbing that the Malverns has to offer.

HISTORY

The vagaries of the 1939-45 war brought various climbers to the Radar Establishments based in Great Malvern and these, together with Wilfred Noyce who was at that time teaching at Malvern College, formed the nucleus of pioneering rock climbers on the Malvern Hills. Few additional new crags or climbs have been discovered since these early days. Interesting documentation of the climbs completed in this period can be found in the 1949 Climbers Club Journal by C.W.F.Noyce and the 1951 M.A.M Journal by R.Chasmer and H.Sutcliffe.

SITUATION AND CHARACTER

The Malvern Hills are composed of diorites and granitic igneous rocks. Natural outcrops of rock occur along the length of the hills but they only exist in appreciable size at the northern end on the slopes of Worcestershire Beacon and North Hill. The naturally outcropping rock is reasonably well weathered and moderately rough whereas the more recent quarried exposures of rock provide a complete contrast being unconsolidated, unsafe and positively dangerous for the climber.

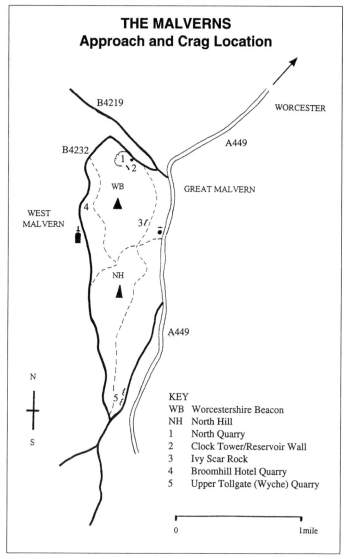

THE MALVERNS
Approach and Crag Location

B4219

WORCESTER

B4232

A449

GREAT MALVERN

WB

WEST
MALVERN

3

NH

A449

N

S

5

A449

KEY

WB   Worcestershire Beacon
NH   North Hill
1   North Quarry
2   Clock Tower/Reservoir Wall
3   Ivy Scar Rock
4   Broomhill Hotel Quarry
5   Upper Tollgate (Wyche) Quarry

0   1mile

ACCESS

All the climbs described in this section lie on land owned and managed by the Malvern Hills Conservators, a body empowered by an act of Parliament and local councils to preserve the hills for all to enjoy. The Conservators have no objection to rock climbing on their land and do not require individuals to seek permission, but they do ask that a courtesy telephone call be made to their office at Priors Croft, Great Malvern (Telephone Number: 01684 892002) prior to a visit.

APPROACHES

From the North, approach can be made south to Worcester by following either the M5 or the A38. Approach to the Malvern Hills from Worcester by following the A449 to Great Malvern and then the B4232 to the Clock Tower Car Park, OS Ref: 770469, Sheet 150 (1:50,000 Landranger Series).

THE CLIMBS

CLOCK TOWER AREA

The Clock Face
   OS Ref: 769470 Sheet 150 (1:50,000 Landranger Series)

Immediately behind The Clock Tower and set above broken rocks is a small headwall with a tree at its centre: **The Clock Face**. The left-hand boundary rib from the base of The Clock Tower can be climbed at a Moderate standard to gain the left-hand end of the wall. The following route is then gained by traversing very carefully rightwards beneath the wall through thick vegetation.

1.   **Wait a Minute**   25ft VS 4B
     Start just to the left of the right-hand arête of the wall and climb trending rightwards to gain the arête near the top. Unprotected.

The flake just to the right has been climbed to provide **Just a Second,** HVS 4B, 25ft; unfortunately, the flake is dangerously loose so climb this only at your peril!

Reservoir Wall

OS Ref: 769469 Sheet 150 (1:50,000 Landranger Series)

This can be approached from The Clock Tower by following the brick steps signposted 'TO NORTH HILL, TABLE AND SUGAR LOAF HILLS'. Follow the continuation path around to the right and then take the right-hand flight of steps to reach Reservoir Green, a grass covered reservoir which is obvious by name. **Reservoir Wall** can be seen as the small outcrop at the far end of this grass reservoir.

There are four routes but the rock is rather shattered and natural protection is not plentiful nor is it particularly reliable. The climbing is steep and the routes are therefore serious undertakings. Top-roping is recommended as a means of making the most of the crag.

The routes are described from RIGHT to LEFT. At the right-hand side of the wall is a prominent deep chimney, to the right of the chimney is;

2. **The Prow**   40ft HVS 5A
   Awkward initial moves up the shallow groove gain undercuts and a thin crack above. Finish via the thin crack with further assistance from the right arête. Tree belay.

3. **Reservoir Cracks**   35ft VS 4B
   A steep route of some historic interest. Start just to the left of the base of the chimney. Climb directly and then move rightwards to gain a standing position on the small nose. Step right and gain the ledge with the sycamore tree. From the left-hand side of the ledge continue carefully up the wall to the top. Stake belay well back behind the stone wall.

4. **Right Groove**   30ft HVS 4C
   Start at the left-hand side of the small slab and some 10ft to the left of the chimney. Climb up to gain the ramp on the right and then move left to gain and finish with difficulty up the shattered groove just right of the small conifer. Tree belay well back.

5.   **Central Groove**   30ft E1 5A
     Strenuous. Start roughly in the centre of the wall, some 20ft
     to the left of the chimney. Climb with difficulty on awkward
     sloping holds to finish up the shallow groove just to the left
     of the small conifer. Tree belay well back.

North Quarry

     OS Ref: 771469 Sheet 150 (1:50,000 Landranger Series)

A large quarry which is approached via the track some 50 yards
beyond The Clock Tower. The quarry is clearly visible from the
approach to **Reservoir Wall.**

     The quarry contains a distinctive lower wall with an obvious
sweeping slab above the terrace. A number of routes have been
recorded here over the years but, without exception, these are
extremely loose and cannot therefore be recommended. The
lower wall is a popular spot for abseiling and is frequently used
by local youths and organised groups.

Ivy Scar Rock

     OS Ref: 773464 Sheet 150 (1:50,000 Landranger Series)

Approach by following the footpath which climbs gently around
the east side of North Hill from the car park at The Clock Tower.
This is a relatively compact outcrop reaching a maximum height
of 50ft and providing several interesting climbs. Unfortunately,
the rock is rather dirty in places and protection is not easy to find.

     The obvious feature of the crag is the slabby corner directly
behind the wooden seat with a steep wall to its left. Stakes are in
place for belays. The climbs are described from LEFT to RIGHT.

6.   **Ivy Buttress**   Hard Severe 4A
     A good route up the left edge of the crag starting at the base
     of the arête. Climb onto the obvious large block at 15ft. Step
     delicately right into a shallow groove which is followed
     before moving left to finish up the easier angled slab.

7. **Ivy Buttress Direct**   VS 4C
    Start at the foot of the arête. Climb the arête to join the original route above the delicate step across.

The steep corner up the middle of the wall to the right of the arête has been top-roped at 5B but, owing to several loose holds and a lack of protection, this has probably not been led.

8. **The Hangover**   HVS 4C
    The obvious slabby corner is taken direct with poor protection and awkward sloping holds. An easier variation, **The Original Route** VS 4B, starts up the slab 10ft to the right to join and finish up the corner.

9. **The Sidle**   Severe 4A
    The obvious rightward-trending diagonal line starting on the lower slab passing under the overhang to finish delicately via a hidden crack.

10. **The Slide**   VS 4B
    Start as for *The Sidle* on the lower slabs and climb directly to finish rather awkwardly up a shallow groove.

11. **Strong Persuader**   HVS 5A
    Start a few feet right of *The Sidle*. Pull straight up to the overlaps, to where *The Sidle* starts to move right, step right and climb the steep wall to the top.

12. **The Sidel**   Hard Severe 4A
    A direct line on dusty, sloping holds to the finish of *The Sidle*.

Upper Tollgate (Wyche) Quarry

OS Ref: 769439 Sheet 150 (1:50,000 Landranger Series)

The highest quarry on the Wyche Road, the A4105, situated some 300 yards down the road on the east side of the Wyche cutting. The quarry floor is used as a car park and there is a corrugated iron-roofed building which serves as a useful landmark.

On the left-hand side of the quarry, behind the corrugated iron-roofed building, there are two obvious slabby grooves lying to the right of a large rockfall. The left-hand groove has a small overlap at approximately two-thirds height. **The Witch**, 75ft, VS 4B, gains this groove at the overlap from the right arête but due to the vegetated and unpleasant nature of the rock this climb has not been checked and cannot be recommended. Some distance to the right and hidden by trees in the centre of the back wall of the quarry is a slabby arête with a twin sycamore tree growing near to its base.

13.   **Tollgate Arête**   120ft E1
After a poor start the slabby arête provides some interesting and very bold climbing on the first pitch.
1.   70ft 5A. Climb the dirty groove on the left and move right to gain the small sapling beneath the overlap. Move delicately left to gain good holds at the base of the arête proper. Climb boldly up the arête, either direct or by starting on the right, to gain an awkward tree belay.
2.   50ft 4B. Climb the cracked wall above the tree to easier broken ground and trend leftwards to a tree belay.

Direct Start. It is possible, though even less desirable, to climb directly on loose rock to gain the sapling beneath the overlap on the first pitch.

Broomhill Hotel Quarry
OS Ref 764465 Sheet 150 (1:50,000 Landranger Series)

A small, sheltered, west-facing quarry which is slow to dry and rather vegetated. Approach by continuing along the B4232, past the Clock Tower, and into West Malvern. About 100 yards south of West Malvern Village Hall on the east side of the road is the Broomhill Hotel. A few yards south of the hotel entrance a footpath leads to a gate. The quarry lies through the gate on the right . The climbs are described from LEFT to RIGHT.

14. **Jennie Said I Could**   25ft Severe
Gain and climb the obvious thin leftward-trending crack moving left at the top to a tree belay.

15. **Syringe**   35ft VS 4C
Follow the previous route until it is possible to step rightwards into the hanging groove. Follow this to a ledge and then move left to a tree belay.

16. **We Know The Meaning Of Cleaning**   40ft Hard Severe
The slabby central groove. Move easily into the smooth upper groove and step right to a ramp leading to a small tree. Move diagonally right to a tree belay.

17. **Smack**   40ft E2 5B
Start just right of the arête. Pull up onto the slab with difficulty and climb past a jammed wire to a ledge on the left. Step back right and finish carefully up the flakes.

THE MALVERN HILLS: FIRST ASCENTS

Details of the following routes are unknown: *The Slide, The Sidel*

The Hangover	H.Sutcliffe, by the original line, 1943
	The direct ascent is traditional.
The Sidle	H.Sutcliffe, 1943
Reservoir Cracks	C.W.F.Noyce and P.F.Holmes, 30/3/49
Ivy Buttress	C.W.F.Noyce, 1949
	Climbed direct by S.Richardson in 1979.
Just a Second	C.W.F.Noyce, 1949
Wait a Minute	C.W.F.Noyce, 1949
The Witch	R.S.D.Smith and T.Southall, 19/5/77
Tollgate Arête	R.S.D.Smith and H.Clover, June 1978
	The direct start was added by R.Lanchbury on 18/7/93.
The Prow	S.Richardson and I.Johnston, June 1978
Right Groove	H.Clover and S.Richardson, June 1978
Central Groove	S.Richardson and H.Clover, June 1978
Strong Persuader	I.Johnston, 1979
We know the meaning etc.	P.Stacey and D.Kerr, 12/7/87
Jennie Said I could	P.Stacey (Solo), 19/9/87
Syringe	R.Lanchbury, T.Penning and A.Norbury, 27/9/87
Smack	T.Penning, R.Lanchbury and P.Cresswell, 27/9/87
	Originally led with a bolt runner. This was removed and led by D.Kerr in October 1987.

Publication of Rock Climbs in the West Midlands. 1988.

OTHER CRAGS

Kinver Edge
OS Ref: 835836 Sheet 138 (1:50,000 Landranger Series)
The edge is well signposted from Kinver Village. The land is owned by the National Trust who have erected 'No Climbing' signs. Climbing at Kinver has taken place mainly on the **Holy Austin Rock**; the sandstone has been carved in many places to provide interesting rock houses which are now mainly used by glue sniffers.

Habberley Valley
OS Ref: 803779 Sheet 138 (1:50,000 Landranger Series)
Habberley Valley lies three quarters of a mile to the north-west of Kidderminster and off the B4190. A signpost 'Private Road Habberley Valley' indicates the entrance to the valley and visitors may drive up the road, but cars must be left in the car park on the right-hand side of the road after approximately 800 yards. Habberley Valley is owned and managed by Wyre Forest District Council and there are no restrictions on climbing.

There are two areas of climbing. **Peckett Rock** is the obvious weathered sandstone pinnacle which offers some interesting bouldering. The clean slabs at the head of the valley, **Ridgestone Rock**, may also provide some amusement, they reach a maximum height of 70ft but are rather friable. The steps cut into Ridgestone Rock are known as **Jacob's Ladder.**

Black Stone
OS Ref: 794740 Sheet 138 (1:50,000 Landranger Series)
A large lump of sandstone situated one mile south of Bewdley and lying behind Black Stone Farm. Black Stone reaches a height of 160ft and the landowner now charges a fee for the use of the crag. Black Stone is mainly used by organised groups for abseil practice and it can offer very little to tempt the serious climber.

Printed by CARNMOR PRINT & DESIGN
95-97 LONDON ROAD, PRESTON, LANCASHIRE, UK.